Siberian Cats as Pets

A Complete Siberian Cat Owner Guide

Siberian Cat Breeding, Where to Buy, Types, Care, Temperament, Cost, Health, Showing, Grooming, Diet and Much More Included!

By Lolly Brown

Foreword

Have you ever thought of getting a cat who was popular in fairy tales before you were even born? Look no further than the Siberian cat, Russia's national cat and national treasure. This breed has lived for a long time, existing in the wild, honed by mother nature to survive the severe Russian climate, is a hunter, and a survivor. These days, the Siberians are making a killing at cat shows, and they have won their way into people's hearts the world over.

One of the things that draw people to this cat is the allegedly hypoallergenic coat that is good for those who suffer from cat allergies. But while "hypoallergenic" cat is really a myth, the Siberian does satisfy some people who marvel at the discovery that they suffer no allergic reactions to the Siberian's fur. And thus begins a long friendship with a gorgeous and wonderful feline.

If you ever thought of getting a Siberian cat, it is always a good idea to do your research into what owning a Siberian cat entails. Read on, and enjoy the journey of getting to know one of the oldest breeds of domestic cats in the world!

Table of Contents

Introduction

More formally known as the Siberian Forest Cat, Siberians are steadily gaining popularity among cat lovers the world over. This medium to large cat exists in all coat colors and patterns, and are reputedly still seen in the wild in the taiga forests of Russia, the country where they came from.

This is a strong and hardy cat, powerful, balanced, and a great hunter. Yet the Siberian also has a sweet facial expression. It teaches you some of the things you will gradually learn about your own Siberian cat: they are powerful, muscular, agile, and yes they still retain their capacity for being good hunters. But the expression on their face is genuine, too. This is one of the sweetest, most loving cats around. The thick fur and general roundness of their overall physique also makes them very cuddly, and they make great lapcats for their adoring owners.

These days, owing to the costs of importation, the relatively recent development of the "modern" Siberian cat pedigree, and the limited number of pedigree stock, this cat is still comparatively rare outside of its mother country. We are really only starting to get to know this cat, but most can agree that you never regret having one be a part of your life.

If you have ever thought of becoming the owner of a Siberian cat, then do your research first. Make sure that you have the capacity to take care of this breed, and what it means to bring a Siberian cat home to be part of your family. This book contains many of the information you will be looking for, such as grooming, exercise, diet and nutrition, and health conditions. For the more enterprising readers, we have also included a brief history of the Siberian cat breed, and sections on showing and breeding Siberian cats.

Glossary of Cat Terms

Abundism – Referring to a cat that has markings more prolific than is normal.

Acariasis – A type of mite infection.

ACF – Australian Cat Federation

Affix – A cattery name that follows the cat's registered name; cattery owner, not the breeder of the cat.

Agouti – A type of natural coloring pattern in which individual hairs have bands of light and dark coloring.

Ailurophile – A person who loves cats.

Albino – A type of genetic mutation which results in little to no pigmentation, in the eyes, skin, and coat.

Allbreed – Referring to a show that accepts all breeds or a judge who is qualified to judge all breeds.

Alley Cat – A non-pedigreed cat.

Alter – A desexed cat; a male cat that has been neutered or a female that has been spayed.

Amino Acid – The building blocks of protein; there are 22 types for cats, 11 of which can be synthesized and 11 which must come from the diet (see essential amino acid).

Anestrus – The period between estrus cycles in a female cat.

Any Other Variety (AOV) – A registered cat that doesn't conform to the breed standard.

ASH – American Shorthair, a breed of cat.

Back Cross – A type of breeding in which the offspring is mated back to the parent.

Balance – Referring to the cat's structure; proportional in accordance with the breed standard.

Barring – Describing the tabby's striped markings.

Base Color – The color of the coat.

Bicolor – A cat with patched color and white.

Blaze – A white coloring on the face, usually in the shape of an inverted V.

Bloodline – The pedigree of the cat.

Brindle – A type of coloring, a brownish or tawny coat with streaks of another color.

Castration – The surgical removal of a male cat's testicles.

Cat Show – An event where cats are shown and judged.

Cattery – A registered cat breeder; also, a place where cats may be boarded.

CFA – The Cat Fanciers Association.

Cobby – A compact body type.

Colony – A group of cats living wild outside.

Color Point – A type of coat pattern that is controlled by color point alleles; pigmentation on the tail, legs, face, and ears with an ivory or white coat.

Colostrum – The first milk produced by a lactating female; contains vital nutrients and antibodies.

Conformation – The degree to which a pedigreed cat adheres to the breed standard.

Cross Breed – The offspring produced by mating two distinct breeds.

Dam – The female parent.

Declawing – The surgical removal of the cat's claw and first toe joint.

Developed Breed – A breed that was developed through selective breeding and crossing with established breeds.

Down Hairs – The short, fine hairs closest to the body which keep the cat warm.

DSH – Domestic Shorthair.

Estrus – The reproductive cycle in female cats during which she becomes fertile and receptive to mating.

Fading Kitten Syndrome – Kittens that die within the first two weeks after birth; the cause is generally unknown.

Feral – A wild, untamed cat of domestic descent.

Gestation – Pregnancy; the period during which the fetuses develop in the female's uterus.

Guard Hairs – Coarse, outer hairs on the coat.

Harlequin – A type of coloring in which there are van markings of any color with the addition of small patches of the same color on the legs and body.

Inbreeding – The breeding of related cats within a closed group or breed.

Kibble – Another name for dry cat food.

Lilac – A type of coat color that is pale pinkish-gray.

Line – The pedigree of ancestors; family tree.

Litter – The name given to a group of kittens born at the same time from a single female.

Mask – A type of coloring seen on the face in some breeds.

Matts – Knots or tangles in the cat's fur.

Mittens – White markings on the feet of a cat.

Moggie – Another name for a mixed breed cat.

Mutation – A change in the DNA of a cell.

Mutation Breed – A breed of cat that resulted from a spontaneous mutation; ex: Cornish Rex and Sphynx.

Muzzle – The nose and jaws of an animal.

Natural Breed – A breed that developed without selective breeding or the assistance of humans.

Neutering – Desexing a male cat.

Open Show – A show in which spectators are allowed to view the judging.

Pads – The thick skin on the bottom of the feet.

Particolor – A type of coloration in which there are markings of two or more distinct colors.

Patched – A type of coloration in which there is any solid color, tabby, or tortoiseshell color plus white.

Pedigree – A purebred cat; the cat's papers showing its family history.

Pet Quality – A cat that is not deemed of high enough standard to be shown or bred.

Piebald – A cat with white patches of fur.

Points – Also color points; markings of contrasting color on the face, ears, legs, and tail.

Pricked – Referring to ears that sit upright.

Purebred – A pedigreed cat.

Queen – An intact female cat.

Roman Nose – A type of nose shape with a bump or arch.

Scruff – The loose skin on the back of a cat's neck.

Selective Breeding – A method of modifying or improving a breed by choosing cats with desirable traits.

Senior – A cat that is more than 5 but less than 7 years old.

Sire – The male parent of a cat.

Solid – Also self; a cat with a single coat color.

Spay – Desexing a female cat.

Stud – An intact male cat.

Tabby – A type of coat pattern consisting of a contrasting color over a ground color.

Tom Cat – An intact male cat.

Tortoiseshell – A type of coat pattern consisting of a mosaic of red or cream and another base color.

Tri-Color – A type of coat pattern consisting of three distinct colors in the coat.

Tuxedo – A black and white cat.

Unaltered – A cat that has not been desexed.

Chapter One: Understanding Siberian Cats

It is always best to do your research before bringing any cat home. Siberian cats, on the average, live for some 11-15 years, though there are reports of Siberians who have passed the 25 year mark!

This means that your Siberian kitten is going to be a part of your life for a very long time. Such a personal investment on your part requires some forethought, the first of which is: Are you going to be able to give your Siberian cat the kind of life it needs and deserves? In general, Siberians are pretty low maintenance cats, but they do need care, affection, and attention, and it is a poor cat owner who is at least not fully informed about the growing concern about feline diet and nutrition. These are just some of the things that you will have to learn about if you are to bring a Siberian home.

This book contains much of the information you will need in deciding whether or not a Siberian is the right breed of cat for you. But of course you cannot learn everything from a book, or from reading for that matter. Much of what you will learn about your cat, your Siberian will teach you himself, over the course of the rest of his life.

Facts About Siberian Cats

There are a few things you should know about Siberian Forest Cats. The first is that while they are generally low maintenance in terms of grooming, they have a crowning glory of abundant fur that comes in a waterpoof, triple coat, and this does require some attention. The Siberian's coat is comparatively low in allergens compared to other cats, but they do molt - at least twice a year. So unless you have kept up with regular brushing and grooming, you'll likely find yourself with a molting cat, hair everywhere, and a growing problem with matting and tangled fur.

The second is that Siberians are slow to mature. It usually takes them up to five years before they are full growth. This is a medium to large cat breed, so don't be surprised if you find your cat just keeps on growing, and growing, and growing, for the first few years of his life.

And finally, while this cat developed naturally, honed by natural conditions in the Russian wild, and is a magnificent hunter and predator, the Siberian is also a very loving, affectionate, loyal, and gentle cat. In fact, there are those who marvel at this breed's dog-like qualities. The Siberians love keeping company with their owners, and they make perfect lap cats. They are also quite calm and placid, and you'll probably be surprised how such a furry bushy cat can suddenly surprise you with his array of sweet meows, trills, and chirps. And of course, endless purring.

This is an intelligent breed, and they are quite trainable. They have the capacity to master a great number of commands and tricks for the patient owner-teacher. They are quite agile, playful, and certainly loving. Is it any wonder that they are fast becoming a favorite breed among cat enthusiasts and cat shows around the world?

They come in all colors and coat patterns, and are characterized by a general roundness in shape. This is on account both of their abundant triple fur, as well as the solid, muscular physique. They are pretty agile, and generally healthy. So far, Siberians have been shown to be prone to only one genetic disease, and if bred responsibly, you might find yourself getting a Siberian kitten who will be part of your life for a very long time.

Summary of Siberian Cat Facts

Pedigree: the result of careful breeding and development of the erstwhile natural "Siberian" cats that were well-known for years in Russia

Breed Size: medium to large size

Weight: 4-10 kg. (8.8-22 lbs.)

Body Type: hefty; solid and muscular

Coat Length: moderate to long, heavy triple coat

Coat Texture: can be soft or very coarse; longer and thicker fur on the shoulders and chest, curly but not wavy coat on the legs and belly, and a full mane on the chest

Color: wide variety of colors and patterns

Eyes: large, slightly oval in shape, but with a rounded lower line, set wide apart and are slightly oblique; colors can range from coppers to greens, and blue in Neva Masquerade varieties

Ears: medium to large, wide-set, rounded tips with a forward tilt; tufts of fur from the inside of the ears and on the tips, giving them "lynx tips"

Tail: medium length, wide at the base and with a blunt tip; thickly covered with fur from the base to the tip

Temperament: loyal, affectionate, friendly and playful, often being described as having a "dog-like temperament

Strangers: friendly with strangers

Children: very good with children

Other Pets: gets along with dogs and most other pets

Exercise Needs: needs some daily exercise, either playing or walking

Health Conditions: generally healthy but prone to Hypertrophic cardiomyopathy (HCM), Polycystic Kidney Disease (PKD)

Lifespan: wide range, average 11 to 15 years

Siberian Cat Breed History

The history of the Siberian cat can be approached in two stages: the second stage centers mainly around the development of the modern Siberian cat as we know it today. This started around 1987 after the first cat show in Russia and the beginning of the development of the Siberian as a pedigree breed.

But prior to this time - one might say ages before this time - the Siberian cats were already pretty well-known in Russia. Before breed standards and feline pedigrees, they were known mainly as "the fluffy cats" to Russians. This is a natural breed that adapted and evolved over time to their natural environment, in relative isolation to cat populations from other regions (i.e., "landrace"). It is thought to be closely related to the Norwegian Forest Cat, and is even said to be the ancestor of all modern long-haired cats, though it is more probable that all modern long-haired cats such as the Angora and the Persian share the same ancestors with the Siberian. The Siberian, though, certainly evolved in its own unique way - by acclimatizing itself to the cold and snowy Russian climate.

The Siberian is ancient, and the earliest records of this magnificent cat can be traced back to as early as 1000 AD. Since then, they have figured prominently in the popular consciousness of the local population - in Russian folktales and fairy tales, they were known as protectors of the elderly and of children, and are able to open gateways to magical realms. Many were feral, or existed in the wild, others were strays, while there were some domesticated Siberians that grew close to their adoptive families and dutifully performed mouse catching duties.

Interestingly, the name "Siberian" is a bit of a misnomer. Perhaps it has to do with some of the folklore associated with this natural breed - as cats that were said to have descended from wild forest cats from the dense, snowy forests of the taiga, or as cats that guarded the monasteries in Siberia during the Middle Ages. Or perhaps it was the unique, triple coat that one easily associates with the severe snowy climate of Siberia. There is no actual evidence or documentation, in any case, to show that the Siberian cats originated from Siberia, or were endemic to North East Russia, as they were could be seen pretty much everywhere in the country. Among the stray cats, those with thicker and waterproof coats had better chances of surviving the climate, so these were naturally more prevalent.

But no one can really point to a specific breed that can be characterized as a "Siberian." One interesting anecdote is post-war Leningrad after the 872-days siege. The city was devastated, and many of the population, including the cats, died of hunger and cold. It was fertile ground for the invasion of rats, which people later sought to counter by bringing in cats from all over the USSR. These cats were brought to the Russian capital by train, and thus cats of all possible types mixed, including, of course, the long-haired fluffy cats known as the Siberian. Though the mixture of thousands of these cats naturally resulted in many different types.

In the 1980s, the cat fancy hit Russia and the USSR, and shows took place in large cities such as Riga, Moscow, and Leningrad. Many people poured into these shows, bringing along their cats, and various breeds were identified among these household pets, but of course nobody could consider them purebreeds yet. And so the idea for a Russian cat breed was born. Naturally it had to be a distinctive cat, and while "Siberian cats" were certainly considered, nobody could pinpoint what precisely were the Siberian cats among the local cat population. The efforts at developing the Siberian cat as a distinct breed were undertaken by different cat breeders and fanciers, but it was the Kotofei Club, through its president Olga Mironova and assisted by Irina Katzer, that wrote and publicized the first written standard for the breed. This standard was based on two very well-known Siberians: Mars, a blue lynx point and white; and Roman - a brown tabby and white.

Since 1988, the shows brought in foreign judges and cat fanciers, people took great interest in the Siberian, and thus paved the way for the worldwide popularity of this breed. The Siberian's recognition by many of the cat organizations in the world are still fairly recent, owing to the somewhat prohibitive cost of exporting these cats from Russia, including export limitations due to a limited breeding stock, the breed is still comparatively rare elsewhere in the world. In the United States, the first Siberians were imported by Mrs. Elizabeth Terrell of Baton Rouge, Louisiana, and David Boehm of Hackensack, New Jersey in 1990. It wasn't until 2002 that the breed came the Britain, and to Australia in 2003, from the US. Catteries, cat clubs and cat enthusiasts in Russia and all over the world have helped to promote their popularity all over the world.

Today, the Siberian cat is the national cat of Russia.

Chapter Two: Things to Know Before Getting a Siberian Cat

We've gotten to know a little bit about the Siberian cat, its history, its temperament, and what it means to have one be part of your family. But before you take the plunge and bring home a Siberian, it is best to know more about what you are getting into. This chapter contains some of the less romantic, and more practical, information about what it means to keep a Siberian cat. We will look at licensing information, how they are with other cats and pets, and how much it would cost over the next couple of years. Finally, to sum things up, we will look at a brief overview of the pros and cons of this breed

Do You Need a License?

Whether or not you need a license to keep a Siberian cat - or any cat, for that matter - depends on where you live. There is hardly any federal regulation governing pet ownership - most of it is determined at the local level. Check your local state laws. There are some states that mandate cat licenses, and there are corresponding fees or penalties for violations.

Cat licensing usually requires the payment of a fee, and proof of vaccination for rabies. You will then receive license proper documentation and license tags which the cat can wear around his collar - after all, part of the reason for licensing is to allow the easy location of the owners of lost cats. Another option is microchipping - which is helpful if the cat's collar or tags come off for whatever reason. Even if your state does not require cat licenses, it is always a good idea to microchip your cat, or at the very least, provide your name and address on the cat's collar in case he ever does get lost. Feline population is a big problem the world over, and there are many unwanted and homeless cats out there. Just in case your Siberian does get lost, don't let him be part of that statistic. Make sure that he can be traced back to you as easily as possible.

Cat licenses are usually renewed after a period of time, during which you are again required to present proof of recent vaccinations. This is a good way to help you keep track of your cat's vaccinations. If he ever does get lost - you want him kept safe and healthy from all possible diseases he might possibly catch from other cats.

Do Siberian Cats Get Along with Other Pets?

Assuming proper socialization, Siberians get along famously with other cats and other pets such as dogs. When you are bringing him home for the first time, in fact, you might want to make a proper introduction between your Siberian and the rest of your household - including other pets such as dogs. There is no reason at all why a Siberian can't get along with other pets, as they are pretty calm, mild-mannered and gentle creatures.

A word of warning, however, regarding smaller pets such as birds or mice. Don't forget that the Siberian cats evolved in the taiga forests of Russia, and they survived, for the most part, by being hunters. Even the early Siberian cats that lived alongside humans earned their keep as mousers. Siberians, like most cats, can have a strong hunting instinct that they will probably keep for the rest of their lives. If you do have smaller pets inside the house, exercise due caution, and never leave them together unsupervised.

How Many Siberian Cats Should You Keep?

Whether or not you decide to keep more than one Siberian cat is really up to you. It might be a good thing if, for instance, you spend most of your time outside the house. While Siberians are not needy, they are affectionate, and they will not appreciate being left alone for long periods of time. They might grow bored and uninterested for lack of enough playmates. Then it might be a good idea to provide him some companionship with another Siberian cat to have someone to play with.

But beware that keeping more than one cat in the house can easily double your expenses when it comes to food, litter, and veterinarian expenses. And it doubles the litter cleanup and smell potential, too. Needless to say, it also doubles the grooming time. And if you are keeping one male and one female cat, for goodness sake, have them spayed if you don't intend on breeding. Otherwise, it can get pretty distracting inside your home whenever the female's heat cycle starts up again. Not to mention the surprise of having your female producing unplanned for and unexpected litters of kittens.

How Much Does it Cost to Keep a Siberian Cat?

Now it's time to talk in terms of numbers. How much is this going to cost you? Be aware that you will be shelling out more for your cat during your first year compared to the following years, and that there will be recurring costs each year thereafter. Below is a breakdown of the initial costs (the cost for your first year of ownership), followed by succeeding annual costs.

The initial costs for your Siberian cat include the purchase price - and this pretty much depends on where you purchase your cat. If you are adopting, the costs can range from $100 to 250. But a purebred from a reputable breeder easily costs more, and usually an average of $1,500. Siberian cats are, after all, still quite rare outside of Russia. If it is a Siberian from a quality show line, sometimes a kitten can cost as much as $3,000 to as high as $15,000.

Other costs during your first year include pet equipment and tools such as the cat bed, cage, toys, and other cat accessories such as a scratching post and a perch. You will also have to budget for neutering or spaying, vaccinations, and medical checkups. Also include a good selection of quality grooming tools and equipment. Below is a tentative breakdown of these costs:

- Pet equipment and accessories such as a bed, collar, food and water bowls, grooming accessories, and a good range of cat toys. A good estimate for this is about $250 (£193.05)
- The costs of microchipping your cat can range from around $20-25 (£15.44-19.31).
- Spaying or Neutering, with Veterinarian fees can average anywhere from $130-170 (£100.39-131.27)
- Your cat may come to you already having received their initial vaccinations. Some additional vaccinations might be required, however, and it is a good idea to budged around $50 (£38.61) for this.

Factor in the regular annual expenses of food, litter, flea treatment, worming, vet fees, and where necessary, grooming and insurance expenses.

Below is a table illustrating the projected initial and annual costs of Siberian cat ownership:

Item	Initial Costs	Annual Costs
Initial Purchase Price	$1,000-1,500 (£770-1,155)	
Pet Equipment and Accessories	$250 (£193.05)	
Microchipping	$20-25 (£15.44-19.31)	
Food		$250-310 (£193.05-

		239.38)
Cat Litter		$75-150 (£57.92-115.83)
Veterinarian Fees, Spaying or Neutering	$130-170 (£100.39-131.27)	
Vaccinations	$50 (£38.61)	
Worming		$50-75 (£38.61-57.92)
Flea Treatment		$75 (£57.92)
Veterinarian Fees		$50-65 (£38.61-50.19)
Insurance		$95-235 (£73.36-181.47)
Grooming and other miscellaneous expenses		$250-645 (£193.05-498.07)

*Costs may vary depending on location
**U.K. prices based on an estimated exchange of $1 = £0.77

It is also a good idea to set aside a fair amount for unforeseen pet emergencies such as unexpected medical or veterinarian bills. Also remember that while the above can give you a fair idea of what Siberian pet ownership could cost, it is still only a general estimate, and much really depends on where you live, the costs in your area, and your own choices on what to spend for and what kind and types of tools, equipment, or services you prefer.

What are the Pros and Cons of Siberian Cats?

Finally, we come to a breakdown of the pros and cons of having a Siberian cat in your home. Please be as honest and objective as you can be in evaluating whether or not your home and your lifestyle is a good fit for these cats. For some people, pet ownership is an emotional choice, but if we really want to be able to take care of our Siberian cats, we have to be objective enough to assess whether or not we can take care of them to the extent that they deserve.

Pros for the Siberian Cat Breed

- Siberian cats can be a good choice for those who are prone to cat allergies, due to the lower levels of allergens in their fur
- Siberians have a wonderful temperament: they are playful, agile, intelligent, affectionate, great lap cats, and all around friendly to everyone, including kids and other pets
- Being a highly intelligent breed, Siberian cats can also be trained.

- They might not need to work for their living, but Siberians can be great mouse deterrents as they will pretty much live up to their ancestry of being Russian mousers. As an added bonus, they have also been known to eat spiders and bugs
- Their coat is pretty much low-maintenance. A regular weekly brushing, plus daily brushing during the days when they are molting, should be sufficient grooming.
- This is a pretty hardy and healthy breed. If you get your Siberian from a reputable breeder, and as long as you maintain her health with a good and nutritious diet, chances are that there won't be any major sicknesses in your cat's near future.

Cons for the Siberian Cat Breed

- Siberians shed; or more appropriately, they molt. At least twice each year, you are likely to find an abundance of shed hair everywhere - unless you've kept up with their daily grooming!
- Siberians are an expensive breed, and you have to factor in the expenses and your budget. In the long run, those expenses can really add up!
- Like most cats, they can be destructive on the furniture. You can also pretty much expect regular and daily litter cleanup duties to keep your cat clean and healthy.

- This is not a cat that you can just leave alone for long periods of time. They do need affection and attention. If your lifestyle keeps you out of the house for long periods of time, then perhaps cats aren't a good choice for a pet for you.

- Lastly, don't forget that this is a medium to large breed, so while they can be pretty having been kept as an indoor cat, they will need enough running and playing space inside the house, too. And Siberians are known for being great jumpers, so their living space need not necessarily be limited to the floor space, either.

Chapter Three: Purchasing Your Siberian Cat

The first few chapters have given you a good overview of what Siberian cats are like, and what it means to have them in your home. Based on what we have seen so far, you now have a pretty good idea of whether or not Siberian cats are a good fit for you and your lifestyle.

A word of caution - Siberian cats seem to be the go-to option for those who suffer from cat allergies. This is not necessarily true, however. There is no such thing as a cat that is 100% hypoallergenic. Comparatively speaking, Siberians do seem to have lower allergen levels in their fur, and many allergy sufferers have finally known what it is like to cuddle a cat with Siberians. But this is a cat-to-cat, person-to-person thing. What may be good for others may not be necessarily true for you. Give yourself time to get acquainted with the breed first - perhaps spending a few hours with a Siberian cat owned by a friend to observe your reaction before you make a decision.

Where Can You Buy Siberian Cats?

If your mind is made up that the Siberian is definitely the cat for you, the next step is determining where to purchase your own. It may seem that getting cats for free is always the best thing to do, but this is not necessarily true. Doing your due diligence to begin with is a good way to avoid the heartbreak of getting cute and lovable kittens that end up getting sick and having to be put down.

It is also not a good idea to purchase your cat from pet stores. The truth of it is that reputable breeders will never allow the kittens they have raised since birth to be displayed in cages in pet store windows. The same thing applies - you don't know where these cats came from, who their parents were, and how they were raised. You cannot even be sure that kitty has been dewormed and vaccinated.

So where does that leave us? You have two options: adopting a rescue, or purchasing from a reputable breeder. In both instances, you may want to check the website of the cat organizations nearest your area as they usually carry names of registered breeders, names and addresses of recommended rescues, and sometimes, even specific cats offered for adoption.

Adopting cats from a rescue is always a good and "humanitarian" option and should definitely be considered by those who have enough space in their homes for these unwanted and unloved cats. For one thing, you will be shelling out considerably less money for a rescue - around $200 is pretty cheap when compared to the average of $1,500 or more that purebreed Siberians cost. And rescues at least come with a health certificate, and you will at least have some idea of their background or history, and the expectation that they are current on their vaccines.

A word of warning though: you are not likely to find Siberians in a shelter, and if you do, it is likely to be a mixed breed. Siberians are still a pretty rare breed outside of Russia. The development of the pedigree is relatively recent, and because of the costs of exporting them from Russia, and the low count of breeding stock elsewhere, they are not as common as other purebreds. The first Siberian cats were only brought to the USA around the 90's, and you can expect that those who went to so much trouble bringing them over from across the seas will be pretty careful that none of their brood end up as strays.

Your next option, therefore, is to look for a reputable Siberian cat breeder.

How to Choose a Reputable Siberian Cat Breeder

Just as in the search for a Siberian rescue, it is recommended that you begin your search for a cat breeder using listings provided by your local cat organizations. To be listed, these breeders need to be registered, and they can only be registered if they meet strict standards set down by the cat organizations. If you are unsure how to go about choosing a reputable cat breeder, you can at least rely on the face-value standards set down by virtue of being listed with some international cat organizations that recognize Siberian cats as a pedigree.

But of course the search doesn't stop there. After you've made a list of those living closest to you, the next thing to do is to network. In fact, you are likely to find these breeders in the next cat show - and it is highly recommended that you attend. Many of the pet owners showing cats are breeders - and as they show, you can have a pretty good idea of the kind and quality of cats they have. Talk to them, ask about the possibility of purchasing a kitten from their next litter, and in your conversation, you can probably determine whether or not this breeder has a genuine love for Siberian cats. They will likely be very enthusiastic talking about their cats, and they will enjoy discussing the breed with you. Feel free to ask them all kinds of questions, but be prepared to answers questions, too. If they are reputable and responsible breeders, they will want to know that they will be turning their precious kittens over to a person who knows what they're doing.

You can narrow your selection a bit more by asking if you could visit their cattery, and maybe have a look at the cats. Schedule a visit, and when you're there, pay attention to the following:

- Are the cats kept in clean surroundings? Do they look healthy, well-fed, and content?
- Observe how the breeder deals with the cats. Are they nurturing, loving and affectionate? Or do they mostly shrug off potential problem areas like an uncleaned litter, or scrawny-looking kittens?

Again, don't hesitate to ask questions:

- What food do the cats eat?
- When was their last vaccination?
- When will the kittens be weaned? It shouldn't be earlier than twelve weeks.
- When was the queen's last litter, and when will she be bred again?
- Have the queen and the stud gone through health checks?
- How old are the queen and the stud?
- How long has the breeder been breeding Siberian cats, and how many litters has he/she sold? Is he/she acquainted with how her cats are now doing?

You can probably think of a lot more questions you can ask the breeder to satisfy your curiosity, but perhaps the most important is to ask to see proof of registration. As you converse with the breeder, ultimately, the decision on whether you think this is a good place to purchase a cat is up to you. Be discerning. Remember that you are likely going to have to contact the breeder again sometime - it is always helpful to have an expert available whom you can ask questions - particularly if this is your first Siberian cat; so a breeder you enjoy having a conversation with couldn't hurt.

You will probably be asked to pay a deposit or a reservation fee for your kitten, and this should come with a written contract. Once all the arrangements are finished, settle down for the wait. Kittens should be fully weaned by twelve weeks, so it shouldn't be too long a long wait.

Tips for Selecting a Healthy Siberian Kitten

The day has come: the Siberian kittens are ready to be claimed by their new owners. You head over to the breeder's with some mixture of excitement and trepidation. You hope, of course, that you are getting your money's worth - and find a Siberian kitten that will keep give you good company for many long years.

Well, as to whether the two of you will manage to develop a good cat-owner bond will be primarily up to you and how you take care of the little thing over the long haul. But in selecting your kitten, you can at least know what to look for to ensure that you are picking a good Siberian to work with.

- You don't want a sickly kitten, so look for one that cuddly and round in a healthy way. He should be energetic, playful, curious and active.
- The kitten should have had the beginnings of proper socialization by now, so you should look for a kitten that doesn't shy away from you, and is actually comfortable and confident while being held by a human. Observe, too, how he deals with his mother and his siblings. Proper socialization doesn't just

mean how he interacts with humans, but also with other cats.

- Watch out for unsightly discharges from their nose or the corners of their eyes, too. And be wary when the breeder tells you that some of his/her kittens have had to be separated from the rest of the cats for one reason or another.

As a final note, you can pretty much pick whatever kitten you like, and you can at least be reasonably assured that de-worming, vaccinations, and socialization have been true for all kittens in the litter of a reputable breeder. Some recommend choosing which you like. Others, however, also caution about letting the kittens pick you. You might like the one who pushes forward the most because it seems he must be the one who likes you best, right? Well, taken another way, you will probably end up with a very pushy cat.

Remember that Siberians are a gentle and affectionate breed, and while they do have a measure of dignity and self-confidence, they aren't quite as yowly as other cats. Why not look for kittens who show the beginnings of the kind of Siberian temperament you are looking for in a lifelong companion to begin with?

Preparing Your Home

While you were waiting for the kittens to be weaned, you must have already put some thought into preparing your home for the arrival of your new family member. This means kitten-proofing your home.

Cats - especially kittens - are naturally curious, and unless you are planning to keep an eye on them 24-7, you should clear and organize your home so that the little furball won't end up ripping into some important documents, or worse, ending up in an unintended accident that can prove fatal in the long run.

Aside from preparing their bed, their litter, and the space where they will have all their toys, you should also put some thought into kitty-proofing your home. This is not unlike baby-proofing your home, in fact, with the difference that kittens are a lot more agile. Siberian cats, in fact, are known to be great jumpers. So double care should be taken. Here are a few tips to guide you:

- Secure all the doors and windows so that your cat will not have an opportunity to slip out when you're not looking. Even if you plan for your cat to stay outdoors most of the time, this shouldn't apply to kittens that are still very vulnerable. Keep them safe by keeping them indoors - especially since your home and your neighborhood is still uncharted territory for them.

- Store away breakable, fragile, delicate, and expensive items. You don't want them accidentally tipping these things over, especially if you have a bunch of valuable but breakable items in your home.

- Secure open containers of water, including the toilet lid. Prevent accidental drowning!

- Store cleaning items, your medicine, food, and garbage in a secure place where the kittens cannot get to them. While you're at it, you might want to remove all potentially poisonous living plants from your home.

- Clean up by putting away small objects that can be swallowed by kittens. Of course, this applies to items with sharp edges or points like needles, razors, knives, etc.

- Hide or secure all cords, electrical wiring, floor-length curtains, or even trailing tablecloths. Cats have a penchant for climbing to high places, and they also have a fondness for playing - even chewing - various threads or cords. You don't want them being accidentally electrocuted, or even caught in the cables or cords and accidentally hung.

- And finally, cats and kittens have this thing about getting into strange places. Before you turn on appliances like the dryer or washer, be sure to check inside!

- Keep them away from open sources of fire such as candles or fireplaces. A kitten may have no natural instinct for danger when it comes to man-made things or equipment.

Kitten-proofing depends largely on the kind of home you have. Look around, and try to see your house as a kitten would see it. Do you see anything else that could potentially cause them harm? Then put it away and out of reach.

Chapter Four: Caring for Your New Siberian Cat

MURMUR'S SIBERIAN CAT

Taking care of a Siberian cat means so much more than giving them a home, giving them something to eat, and the occasional grooming. It also means providing them with the opportunity to grow into the best kind of cat they can be.

This means enough space to move around, enough exercise, enough mental and physical stimulation, and plenty of play. Siberians were originally hunters and predators living in the wild, and while your cuddly Siberian makes a good case for the modern life by lounging around and sleeping all the time, neither you nor your Siberian can argue with the peculiar needs of his body and mind - which have been honed by years of development, evolution, and natural selection. He may not spend his life as his ancestors did - chasing mice around the farm. But you do want him to be healthy and fit so that if he wants to, he could.

Habitat and Exercise Requirements for Siberian Cats

The good news is that Siberian cats are adaptable enough that they can thrive indoors just as easily as they can outdoors. They do not need to go oudoors, and it is actually advisable that they not be let outdoors at all - certainly not unsupervised. They may be incredible hunters and capable of surviving in harsh climate and conditions, but this is a far cry from the dangers that the human world can pose for an unsuspecting Siberian.

In fact, statistics show that cats who live outdoors have comparatively short lifespans compared to cats who are kept indoors. Dangers abound outdoors for all cats - from cars and vehicles plying the roads, various food lying around that may be poisonous to your cat, or even people who can demonstrate either cruelty or greed as they catnap expensive-looking outdoor cats. It's best not to risk it.

That said, you might think that the danger for cats kept indoors is the lack of healthy exercise and the possibility of becoming obese - not the mention the questionable health of cats who are never exposed to the outside air and sunlight. But this need not be true. Siberians can make great lapcats, but if you can provide them with enough running space inside the house and a wide range of toys and accessories to play with and to challenge them, they can actually thrive indoors. Some indoor Siberian cats have been known to live for as long as 20+ years!

Toys you can try include lasers, teasers, balls, catnip toys, a good scratching post and high perch, rattles, and mouse toys, among others. Or something as simple as a cardboard box, crumpled pieces of paper, or other simple household items can serve well enough to distract your Siberian cat for a long hour of play. You likely won't have to spend much on toys. But you might want to have a good range available as cats have a penchant of losing interest in something quickly and it would be helpful if there is something else they can turn their attention to.

Of course, it is important that you also spend enough time with your cat - whether in playing, training, or simply cuddling. Cats are affectionate and loyal pets, and Siberian cats more so - some have described them as having dog-like personalities that make them attached to their human families. Create a nurturing environment for them, and make them feel part of the family. They will be living with you for a great many years still, after all.

One other option you can have is to walk your cat. Yes, there are cat owners out there who walk their cats - particularly medium to large-sized cats like the Siberian for whom some outlet to expend their energies is necessary. Get them used to the feel of a collar, leash and harness early on, and take them out for short, periodic walks to begin with. Always keep in mind that it you are responsible for the welfare of your cat once you are outside. For one thing, they have to be on top of their vaccinations so that they don't catch anything from the other cats. Allow them to explore the world and to satisfy their curiosity, but make sure that he does not chew or swallow anything dangerous, that he is not exposed to violent dogs, and that he doesn't get loose from his leash. In fact, you might want to microchip him early on in case he does get loose. Needless to say, you should pay close attention if your cat is a female in heat as she'll likely be attracting more attention from the local toms than you'll find yourself comfortable with. You'll probably want to keep her indoors during this time.

Chapter Five: Meeting Your Siberian Cat's Nutritional Needs

A good and healthy nutritious diet is the cornerstone to a healthy Siberian cat. And yet how do you know which is a good diet for your cat? These days, there are so many varying "expert" opinions that it is hard to tell which is which. In this chapter, we present to you some of the best practices when it comes to feline nutrition and diet, but it is important that you realize that ultimately, the decision of your cat's diet depends on you. Make your choices based on what you have learned, what you feel comfortable with, and most importantly, what is healthy for your Siberian cat.

Make it a habit to be observant whenever you make any changes in your cat's diet, and adjust accordingly. A healthy and well-nourished Siberian cat is muscular, strong, hardy, and playful. And always remember not to make any drastic changes in your cat's diet without giving their stomach and digestive system time to adjust. Don't hesitate to consult your veterinarian for expert recommendations, but do your own homework, too!

The Nutritional Needs of Cats

Cats are obligate carnivores. This means that their nutritional requirements are based largely on meat, much as their natural diet if they are in the wild. It is therefore important for your Siberian's diet to be high in proteins and fats.

Recent research has suggested, in fact, that there is a ceiling at which cats are able to process carbohydrates. The only carbohydrates that cats ingest in their natural diet, if they are in the wild, for example, are those that are found in their prey's stomach. Experts are of the opinion that cat lack the enzymes that would enable them to properly digest carbohydrates. If you are giving him a high-carb diet, then this could possibly lead to problems such as digestive diseases and other conditions such as diabetes and pancreatitis.

Many cat owners out there are, in fact transitioning to a raw meat-based diet. If this appeals to you, it is important that you do your research first. Know what types of meat you can give them, and how they should be prepared. Raw meat is a fertile breeding ground for bacteria, so uninformed experimentation is not recommended as you can actually cause illness in your beloved Siberian.

If you prefer feeding your cat the comparatively convenient packaged cat food, look for meat-based cat food that is appropriate to their age level. You can find some tips on choosing quality cat food in the next section.

How to Select a High-Quality Cat Food Brand

Yes, choosing a good and high-quality cat food can be a daunting and sometimes frustrating task. It is literally the confusion of too many choices, each one claiming to be the best for your beloved feline.

How do you choose? Perhaps the simplest answer to this would be to ask around. Ask other cat owners, especially breeders with a good history of breeding and raising healthy cats. Which cat food do they prefer? They can give you some recommendations to narrow their choices, and you might not even need to look further. It is always a good idea, however, to start learning how to read the label on that cat food you are bringing home. This allows you to make informed choices should you later on decide to shift to a different brand of cat food, because after all, you won't get much information from advertisements alone. And with the notoriety of some cats losing interest in the same food day in and day out, you may find yourself having no choice but to alternate between different cat food brands.

First of all, look for the following:

- A nutritional adequacy statement that tells you the age-appropriateness of the cat food, whether it is for kittens, adult or mature cats, or cats in their senior years.
- Look at the name of the cat food. This usually highlights a key ingredient. It is advisable to look at the first word of the cat food name. This is important because the cat food is then required to contain at least 95% of the named ingredient. For instance,

"Tuna Cat Food" or "Chicken Cat Food." Watch out for qualifiers such as "entree," "dinner," "formula," or statements such as "with tuna/chicken", because while the cat food may contain these meat ingredients, adding them only as qualifiers means that they are not the primary ingredient, and may range from some 3% to anywhere that is less than 95%.

- Next, look at the ingredients list. As much as possible, avoid cat food that contain chicken by products, chicken by-product meal, corn meal, corn gluten meal, wheat gluten. These are not healthy ingredients - as meat by products mostly consist of rendered parts of chicken such as viscera, head, legs, necks and intestines. Corn meal and wheat, on the other hand, are cheap fillers and may even cause indigestion in your cat.

- Not all grain is bad, as rice, rice flour, barley, barley flour, or milled barley can also be a good source of carbohydrates in high quality cat food. Make sure that these are not the primary ingredients, however, as the healthier options are meat-based cat food. Manufacturers are legally mandated to lis ingredients based on their weight in descending order. Look for those that are derived from meats such as chicken, tuna, fish, beef, etc.

- Don't forget to look for a statement that says that the cat food "meets or exceeds AAFCO standards."

Finally, while the choice of whether you give your cat dry or wet food is completely up to you, part of which may even be determined by your lifestyle and how often you are at home - please bear in mind that some experts recommend canned instead of dry kibble. Comparatively, canned food may be preferable because dry kibble has too low water content, too high carbohydrate content, and is mostly plant-based rather than animal or meat-based.

Tips for Feeding Your Siberian Cat

The choice of what to feed your cat is ultimately up to you, but here are a few tips that may guide you:

- Cats are originally desert creatures, and they derive most of their water from the moisture in their food. While you can offer them a constantly filled water bowl at the same time as feeding them dry kibble, they will only occasionally lap up water to make up for their thirst. This means that cats on a steady diet of dry kibble will be in greater danger of dehydration. An alternative is feeding them a mixed diet of dry and canned food.

- Shake it up a bit. If you find a good canned cat food that you think is healthy, it's probably not a good idea to stick to it constantly over the course of his life. For one thing, they might simply become bored with it and lose interest. For another, it's always a good idea to provide them with varied sources of good protein and fats, and the vitamins and minerals that come with either fish or meat. Feeding them too much of one thing can deprive them of important nutrients found in other diets.

- Always provide them with readily accessible clean drinking water. While cats don't have the same sense of thirst that we do, providing them with a good source of clean drinking water allows them to satisfy their thirst whenever they need to, keeping them hydrated and healthy.

- Don't free feed. There is perhaps some leeway for freeding for kittens and pregnant or lactating mothers - these cats need the added nutrients and food for growth and their developmental changes. But for a regular, adult cat - particularly those kept mostly indoors and with limited options for something else to do inside the house - leaving them readily accessible food that they can get to throughout the day opens the doors for obesity in your Siberian. Sure, a rounded furball looks kind of cute and cuddly, but it is fundamentally unhealthy, and can lead to all sorts of illnesses such as diabetes, arthritis, and urinary tract disease.

Dangerous Foods to Avoid

Don't forget that cats are obligate carnivores - and this means a diet completely different from humans and even dogs. So don't think that by giving them what you consider tasty human food you are doing them a favor. Below is a list of some potentially dangerous or even poisonous human foods that a cat should not eat. Take a look around your living space and make sure that none of them are available where your cat can reach them.

- Alcohol
- Candy and Gum
- Chives
- Chocolate
- Coffee
- Dairy Products
- Energy Drinks
- Fat Trimmings and Bones
- Garlic
- Grapes and Raisins
- Mushrooms
- Mustard seeds
- Onions/leeks
- Peach pits
- Potato leaves/stems
- Raw Eggs
- Rhubarb leaves
- Tea
- Tomato leaves/stems
- Walnuts
- Xylitol
- Yeast dough

If your Siberian cat eats any of these foods, contact the
Pet Poison Control hotline right away at (888) 426 – 4435.

Chapter Six: Training Your Siberian Cat

Training your Siberian cat span a great number of things over the course of his life. To begin with, proper socialization during kittenhood is important as this gives him confidence in dealing with his surroundings and with you as his owner. Litter training also gives you both a good understanding when it comes to hygiene and cleanliness, and is going to go a long way in keeping your headaches at a minimum. Lastly, you can also teach your Siberian cat a few tricks and commands. Remember that Siberians are intelligent cats, and they will certainly enjoy training sessions with you if done in a positive and nurturing atmosphere.

Socializing Your New Kitten

The first weeks of a kitten's life can determine his temperament for the rest of his life. You want a confident, well-adjusted cat who isn't afraid of people, of other pets, and of the strange sights and sounds you might find inside your home. Otherwise, all you'll be getting is a constantly stressed out cat.

Socialization takes place early - from the 2nd up until the 12th weeks of age. Many of the things he will learn will come from his mother, but some of it will also come from the breeder. Constant, gentle handling for short periods of time early will help him be accustomed to the presence and handling of humans. And yet, at the same time, it is important not to separate him from his mother too early - many breeders don't do so until the kitten reaches 12 weeks. Any earlier and you will have a kitten who hasn't fully learned what it means to socialize with his mother and his siblings, and likely hasn't learned to groom himself, or even how to use a litter. You'll likely end up bringing home a kitten with anti-social behavior, separation anxiety, and even poor litter box habits.

But while it is recommended that you handle kittens gently and regularly in their first few weeks, neither should you do so for too long periods of time. It is quite possible that the mother might end up rejecting the kitten, and while he may not fear the presence of humans, neither will he learn how to properly socialize with other cats, either.

Socialization is an enjoyable process, but it also requires patience. Once you bring your kitten home, the key is doing things gradually. You might begin by confining him to a single room at first, and slowly introducing him to the rest of the house and the household over the next couple of days. Daily, gentle handling is also important. As your kitten gains confidence in exploring the rest of your house, you can begin exposing him to various stimuli such as different kinds of toys and grooming sessions.

Remember that kittens are curious by nature, and they will want to investigate their surroundings. Encourage this, while at the same time making sure that they are kept safe and are not exposed to any undue danger.

Litter Training for Kittens

For the most part, kittens learn how to use the litter box from their mothers, which is why it is important not to separate them from their mothers too soon. By twelve weeks of age, they should be fully weaned, ready to meet their new owners, and fully acquainted with the niceties of using a litter box.

Your part is to provide the kittens with a clean litter box and good, quality litter. Make sure that the litter box is cleaned regularly, as some Siberians can be finicky enough that they won't like using a smelly or dirty box - much like humans who don't like using a dirty and smelly toilet.

It is a good idea to have at least two litter boxes provided - some cats don't like peeing in the same box as they use for their poop. If you have more than one cat in the house, there are those who don't like to share. Be attentive, and keep their boxes clean! Scoop at least twice a day if possible. Not only does this keep down the smell of feline pee and poop, but it also goes a long way in helping your Siberian maintain the cleanliness of his luxurious coat and fur.

Obedience Training

Like most cats, Siberians are an intelligent breed. Done right, they can be trained to perform various tricks. They aren't quite like dogs who will be quite eager to please - cats are more dignified than that. But Siberians have a strong sense of loyalty and affection for their owners, and with the proper motivation, you can challenge their intelligence and stimulate their mind by teaching them some tricks.

Cats can learn all sorts of tricks - although of course you can begin by teaching them some basic commands such as responding to their name, and to the word "Come." Later on, you can expand your pet's repertoire by teaching them to sit, shake hands, roll over, ring a bell, and various other simple tricks.

You can use treats as a motivation, or you can explore the effectivity of the clicker training method - each time your cat follows one of your commands, use a clicker to signal that it is good behavior, and then reward her with a treat. Done consistently and over time, she will gradually learn to associate the sound of the clicker with desirable behavior.

Remember that cats will likely not appreciate being made to keep still for too long, so keep your training sessions short. Just remember to be patient, and if his attention begins to wander, move on and start again the next day.

Try not to teach more than one trick at a time. Over time, you'll probably be surprised at his capacity of learning a great number of tricks!

Chapter Seven: Grooming Your Siberian Cat

For Siberians, their distinctive coat is their crowning glory. This is a medium-long haired breed with a heavy, triple coat that molts at least twice a year, and also grows thicker during winter time. For any prospective owner of a Siberian cat, knowing how to take care of this cat's gorgeous coat is a must. Regular grooming not only keeps this cat looking his best, but it also prevents the development of troublesome matting and tangling in the Siberian's abundant fur.

The Siberian Triple Coat

Part of the adaptive quality of the Siberian is their coat - the thickness of it allows them to survive the frigid winters of their home country, Russia. They have three types of feline fur: guard hairs, awn hairs, and down. Their fur is textured, but glossy, with an overcoat that is slighly hard to the touch and is also waterproof.

At least once or twice a year, Siberians moult: once after winter, and another "mini-moult" at the end of summer. They also develop a thick winter coat during the end of the year, and this applies even to modern Siberians that are mostly kept indoors and are not exposed to changing seasons. The Siberian's winter coat also features a well developed shirtfront, full frills, and knickerbockers. The summer coat, on the other hand, is distinctively shorter.

Many that eventually choose to keep and raise Siberian cats do so because their coats are allegedly hypoallergenic, which should be good for those with allergies. Strictly speaking, however, this is not quite true. There is no cat breed that is 100% hypoallergenic, although it seems that the Siberian's fur does have lower levels of allergens which cause allergic reactions among people. Cats generally lick their coat when they self-groom, and when their saliva dries, it can fall off as dander, causing allergic reactions to some people. But it seems that Siberians have lower levels of the enzyme Feld1 in their saliva, so there may still be hope for some allergy sufferers. Ultimately, however, it really depends on the specific cat and the person. It is estimated that around 75% of those who have tested themselves out with Siberians have had little or no allergic reaction. If you do have allergies and are thinking of getting a Siberian cat, you might want to test things out for a few hours or so first, just in case.

Tips for Bathing and Grooming Siberian Cats

Siberians are not high-maintenance cats in terms of grooming. If you arm yourself with quality grooming tools and give them a good brushing at least once a week - then stepping things up to daily grooming during molting season, this really should be enough.

Good grooming tools to have include a slicker brush and a metal toothed comb to tease out knots or tangles, and a soft brush to finish up. Start out by stroking your cat to determine if their are any knots or tangles. You usually won't find any since a Siberian cat's coat has natural oils to help maintain his fur, but if you do find some matting, use the comb to tease the knot apart. Don't pull, since this can be painful for your cat. If the knot is tight, start at the ends farther from the skin, and begin detangling, but as gently as possible.

Work your way through his coat. When there aren't any mats or tangles, comb through his coat from head to tail, going with the direction of the hair growth. Doing this once a week gets rid of most of the shedding hair, stimulates the natural oils in the skin, and also serves to relax your Siberian. This is a great bonding time for you and your cat. Finish up with a soft brush all over. You'll might find that this last brushing is particularly pleasurable to your cat, as it approximates maternal licking and grooming.

During molting season, which can last about 10 days, you'll find the hair starting to mat and shed in large clumps. How profuse the shedding is depends largely on each individual cat, but you should adopt daily brushing during this time to help the molting along, and to prevent the matting of his fur. You can use the bristle brush to good effect at this time, and large clumps of molting fur will come off with the brush.

Siberian cats do love water, and while for some this means they also love bathing, this is not necessarily true for all cats. In fact, unless you've gotten them used to bathing, grown Siberians are likely not to appreciate the bath. Unless you're showing, your cat might not need a bath anyway. Regular grooming and brushing sessions is all that is really needed.

If you do decide that it is a good idea to bathe your cat - perhaps they are still kittens and you want them to get used to baths, or perhaps you intend to enter him in the show circuit later on, make sure to use quality cat shampoo. If your cat seems unappreciative of his bath, let him go and try again another time. Forcing him when he clearly wants to be elsewhere will only ruin the experience for him, and it will be doubly difficult to get him into the bath next time. Besides, bathing too often can actually strip their coat of its natural oils. With enough patience and time, you'll find your Siberian appreciating his occasional bath - some Siberians are reputed to love the water so much that they even attempt to join their owners in the shower!

The only reminder for bathing a Siberian is to make sure that you have rinsed their coat thoroughly. They have a very thick fur, and it is essentially waterproof, so bathing them and getting the shampoo in can be a challenge, but rinsing the shampoo off is doubly more so. Half of the bathing time can be spent in rinsing, but this is not something that you should do half-heartedly, either. Remember that cats will groom themselves, so they might just lick off the residue of the shampoo from their coat and ingest it if traces were left in their coat. Dry him off with a towel and a dryer set on low heat.

An easier and gentler alternative to bathing, and possibly more enjoyable for both you and your cat - is to use soft kitty wipes - to give their coat a gentle bath, and is particularly helpful in cleaning their face and nose. Wipe off any discharges in the corners of his eyes and any dirt from his nose and whiskers.

And last but not least, don't forget to keep their litterbox clean. Doing so can go a long way in helping your cat keep his coat clean and hygienic.

Other Grooming Tasks

To complete grooming your Siberian, there are other grooming tasks to finish off your cat's sharp and spiffy look. This includes trimming their nails, cleaning his ears, and brushing his teeth.

Trimming Your Cat's Nails

Make sure you get a quality cat nail trimmer - don't use human nail clippers since these are not designed for cat claws, and can actually injure or ruin their claws. Just squeeze their paws until the claws are revealed - and clip! Just don't trim too much of the claw or you will end up cutting the quick, or the flesh underneath the nail. You can see this quite clearly if their claws are white, but for darker claws, just trip conservatively along the edge.

There are some pet owners who prefer declawing their cats, but some organizations like the CFA does not recommend this, and in fact considers it as a disqualification among show cats.

Cleaning Your Cat's Ears

Always be gentle when cleaning your cat's ears - these are very sensitive and using the wrong tools, such as a q-tip, can potentially hurt or damage their ear canal. Use instead some liquid ear cleaner on a clean cotton ball or a piece of gauze. Clean the inside of your cat's ears gently, lifting away any debris or earwax that you can see.

Make it a habit to examine your cat's ears at least once a week. Be on the lookout for dark-colored debris, a strange odor, excessive wax, discharges, redness or swelling. If you do find any of these in your cat's ears, it is recommended that you have him checked by a veterinarian. It is quite possible that he may have ear mites or some form of ear disease. Regular weekly ear cleaning should help to prevent these diseases from starting in the first place.

Brushing Your Cat's Teeth

While regular brushing is recommended, a good weekly dental care is good enough. Use good cat toothpaste and toothrbush. This keeps their breath smelling fresh and clean, and can go a long way in keeping your cat healthy - staving off dental disease, gum disease, tooth decay, and even heart disease!

You might want to start them out when they're kittens - having a foreign object rubbing against their teeth is not something cats are used to, so it might take a few tries before they finally get used to the idea of having their teeth brushed. If you start them out young, the habit of it will grow on them as they mature, and even if they never grow fond of it, they will at least learn to tolerate it.

If you are dealing with an adult Siberian, however, perhaps using a cat toothbrush is too much of a strange thing for them. An alternative is simply using some microfiber washcloths, which you can use in the same way as a toothbrush. Make sure it is wet with warm water, and use a finger to guide the cloth along your cat's teeth and gums.

Chapter Eight: Breeding Your Siberian Cat

Breeding Siberian cats is a huge responsibility and should not be undertaken lightly. The entire process is likely to consume much of your time, dedication, energy, and money, so it isn't the kind of thing you should enter into half-heartedly, or without a good idea of what you are getting into. Responsibility for other living animals shouldn't be something that you enter into because of a whim. Knowing all this, if you don't plan to breed your Siberian cat, then you should do the responsible thing and have your cat altered, preferably before her first heat at around six months. Doing so can also reduce her risk of getting mammary cancer.

If you are set on breeding your Siberian, be aware that it is going to be a learning experience for you. You should do your part and read, learn, and ask questions. This chapter provides you with a basic background of the feline heat cycle, the breeding process, pregnancy, queening, and raising kittens, all of which you will need to undertake if you plan to breed. Use this book as a starting point or guide, and seek out more information if there are things you still don't understand. Responsible breeders are committed to the health and wellbeing of the mother and her kittens from pregnancy up until they find good homes for the fully weaned kittens, so it will also require a bit of dedication on your part.

Undertaken properly, however, breeding your Siberian can be a most rewarding experience. Not only will you learn more about this lovable cat breed, but you will also have the satisfaction of having reared an excellent litter of tiny Siberians that people will fall in love with.

Basic Cat Breeding Information

It is typically recommended that any prospective breeder begin by showing cats. In fact, when you join the cat show circuit, you might notice that many of those who show are cat breeders. That is because this is an excellent starting point for you to learn more about the breed, their unique quirks and traits, their temperament, and what it means to breed responsibly. In a way, perhaps the dedication required in showing cats is also a good starting point for the dedication required of breeders.

Perhaps one of the most important thing you will learn from showing is the importance of proper selection of the breeding stud and queen. While Siberians are generally healthy, some have been shown to be genetically predisposed to Hypertrophic Cardiomyopathy (HCM), which is the leading cause of heart disease in cats. You don't want HCM being passed on to the kittens, so any cat diagnosed with HCM should not be bred. And of course, based on the breed standards of the cat organizations or show you are joining, you will likely be selective in your selection in terms of ideal Siberian breed standards. This, of course, is simply another facet of breeding to promote the best of the breed.

Comprehensive health checks should be done for both the queen and the stud. Both of them should be at the proper age to breed - neither too young nor too old. Both should at least be 18-24 months before they are bred.

As a final note, when breeding pedigreed cats, registration papers will be important for both the owner of the stud and the owner of the queen. This is because experienced breeders will want to avoid interbreeding, or breeding cats that are too closely related, since this could lead to some serious health problems. Choose cats from the Active Register whenever possible, as there are reasons why some cats are listed as Non-Active, or not recommended to be bred.

The Feline Heat Cycle

Breeding require a good knowledge of the feline heat cycle. This is important because if left unsupervised, cats can breed really fast and really easy, sometimes as early as six to ten months old, which is soon after the female reaches her first heat cycle. This is far too young to keep the female cat healthy, and is also the reason why overpopulation - especially among stray cats - is a big problem.

Cats are seasonally polyestrus, which means that they can come into heat several times during a year, usually in the spring and summer, though some may cycle multiple times during a calendar year. Cycling is initiated by increased daylight, but indoor cats who are exposed to trong artificial light can potentially cycle year round. And cats will continue cycling repetitively until they breed, so you might find a number of toms hanging around outside your door several times in weekly succession if your cat is not bred. The feline's heat cycle usually involves a repetitive cycle of fertility and sexual receptivity, which are driven both by seasons and hormones.

The cat's heat cycle happens in stages. The first stage, or proestrus, can last anywhere from 1-4 days. This will involve some behavioral changes in your female cat. You might find her rubbing constantly against furniture or against your leg, yowling or persistently vocalizing (calling), licking her genital region, or raising her hindquarters and moving her tail from side to side (lordosis). Sometimes there will be a clear discharge from her vagina, increased urination, and she may spray on some vertical surfaces. Of course, some cats may not display any of this calling behavior, and they are what are known as silent callers. What does seem constant is a certain restlessnes and a need to escape and get out of the house to find a mate. During proestrus, however, there will be no mating, and the female will usually prevent this by holding her tail between her hind legs to indicate her lack of receptivity.

The second stage, or estrus, is when actual breeding or mating takes place. She finally becomes receptive to sexual activity, and this can last for an average of 7 days. Mating itself may last for only 1-20 seconds, but during estrus, the queen will allow multiple toms to mate with her, and mating can take place repeatedly over the next 24-48 hours, so it is not uncommon for a litter to be fathered by more than one tom. This is referred to as superfecundity.

Cats are induced ovulators. This means that the act of breeding stimulates ovulation. Repeated breeding thus ensures ovulation. It is important during these initial stages that you manage to confine your queen to the house to avoid her mating with other cats. Once estrus starts, you may want to leave her and the stud alone for as long as she allows mating. The success of breeding varies, but in some queens, it may take several matings before ovulation is induced. You may want to provide sufficient room and board for both the queen and the stud during this time, as repeated mating will likely ensure greater chances of ovulation and pregnancy.

If a cat is not bred, a cat's heat cycle will become longer and more frequent. It is never wise to allow a queen to call three times in succession without being bred. Aside from increasing the chances of cysts forming in her ovaries, it may lead to simultaneous release of all the mature eggs she had been carrying up to that point, and which were never released for lack of breeding. This can lead to difficulties of her carrying too large a litter, or the production of "old" eggs that can result in congenital defects in the kittens.

During the time when your queen is not in heat and you do not think she is ready for pregnancy and motherhood, you should learn the best ways of managing your cat's fertility. As her cycle will only repeat every two or three weeks (sometimes sooner) if she is not bred, you can only keep her confined inside the house for so long. Some ways of managing fertility include:

- Hormone use
- Mechanical stimulation
- Service by a vasectomized male

Consult with your veterinarian as to the pros and cons of each of the methods recommended above.

If a cat is not bred, she enters an interval called interestrus, which lasts for some 2-3 weeks (sometimes sooner), before entering a new heat cycle. If she was bred but did not become pregnant, she enters a stage called diestrus, in which there is no reproductive activity. If the mating was successful, however, the pregnancy will last for an average of 63 days.

Pregnancy and Queening

You often can't tell whether or not your cat is pregnant until she is already a few weeks into her pregnancy, or at 3-4 weeks. By this time, you might notice any of the following signs:

- nipples becoming more pink and prominent
- a baby bump is becoming noticeable
- "morning sickness" such as lack of appetite or vomiting

If you do suspect a pregnancy, bring her to the vet. Confirmation can be done in various ways, such as an feeling the cat's belly, an ultrasound, or an x-ray late during the pregnancy.

Once pregnancy is confirmed, you might want to discuss any recommended dietary changes with your vet. In general though, her appetite should increase gradually and during the sixth week, you might increase her daily diet by 25%. It is important that she get sufficient calories and calcium during this time, and some recommend feeding her a diet that is designed for kittens or growing cats. Some also recommend daily moderate exercise such as walking or playing in order to avoid the potential risk of obesity. She will be eating a lot more as her pregnancy progresses, and some form of regular exercise can help maintain her muscle tone and avoid too much weight gain.

Avoid giving medication to pregnant cats, and ensure, as much as possible, that she is free of parasites such as fleas, ear mites, and roundworms - which can either compromise the health of the kittens, or which may be passed on to the newborns. Bring her to a vet for regular checkup to ensure her good health.

Around two weeks before she is due, begin to prepare her nesting box. Keep this in a safe and secluded area, separate from the other pets in the house. You might notice that during this time, she begins to enter her nesting mode and begins to act differently, such as seeking a secluded place, loss of appetite, and acting restless or fidgety. By this time, you should have gotten her accustomed to her nesting box so that she feels comfortable with it. You can do this during the last weeks of pregnancy, although some cats might still prefer to sneak away somewhere to have their kittens on their own, and you'll end up surprised to find her having given birth inside the closet or elsewhere inside the house. Signs of impending labor are a sudden loss of appetite, and a drop in temperature below 100F. Keep a close eye on her when you notice either.

Most cats know instinctively what to do during labor, or what is termed as "queening," and you might not have to intervene at all. All the same, it is a good idea to stand by and be present during the process, in case things go wrong. If this is your first cat pregnancy, it is probably a good idea to have an experienced breeder with you who can guide you through the entire process. Consult with them early on as to which tools or equipment to have on hand, even if you might not need them. You might want to prepare the following:

- clean towels
- sterile surgical disposable gloves
- dental floss in case you need to help the mother-to-be with cutting the umbilical cords.
- scissors

Have the vet's number and local emergency services at hand to call if things go wrong. Some problem signs to watch out for include discolored discharges, or straining on the part of your cat without kittens being produced.

Labor can last anywhere from 2-5 hours. If you notice that she is having some difficulty, contact your vet. If there are some kittens who are not suckling, try to lead them gently to one of the mom's teats. If all goes well, however, try not to interfere too much, however, as some cats may not appreciate this so soon after giving birth.

Breeding Tips and Raising Kittens

If all went well during the queening or birth, you should allow the mother and her newborns some space for the next 24-48 hours, without bothering her, interrupting her, or attempting to help her with the cleaning. She will require this time to bond with, clean up, and settle her kittens and herself. Try to make sure, at the very least, that the kittens are kept warm. Newborn kittens are unable to regulate their body temperature, and it is dangerous for them to get a chill. Make sure they are not exposed to any drafts, and provide as much clean towels as they would need.

Cats are generally good mothers, and she will raise her litter quite well on her own. She will clean them up, feed them, nurture them, keep them warm, and will eventually wean them and even teach them how to use the litter box. Very little input is needed from you, other than regular gentle handling for socialization, and regular weighing to ensure their proper growth. You can probably expect a daily weight gain of at least 10 grams.

Consult with your veterinarian in case of the following:

- kittens that are weak, malnourished, and not gaining enough weight
- If some of the mother's teats appear red and swollen, have abnormal discharges

You will need to maintain the increased diet for the mother while she is lactating to help her produce enough milk for her kittens. Making sure that the kittens have their mother's first milk, or colostrum, within the first 12 to 24 hours after birth ensures that the newborns also receives their mother's antibodies, thus strengthening their immunity. Try and make sure that all the kittens have their share.

Kittens are completely helpless at birth, and are fully dependent on their mother. After about a week, their eyes will begin to open, though it isn't until a few weeks later that their vision begins to clear. During the second week, they will try to stand and walk, and their sense of sight and hearing will begin to develop. They will begin to explore around the third week, and their teeth begin to develop. It is around the 4th to 7th week that they begin to use the litter box, and by this time they should be quite active and playful.

Weaning typically begins at about 4 weeks, when their teeth have developed enough that they can begin to nibble. Normally, the mother herself will ensure the weaning of her kittens, and you will find that they begin to share in the mother's food around this time. You can assist them in this process by providing them a mixture of dry food mixed with formula to make slush or moistened dry food. At 5-6 weeks, they can begin attempting dry food, such as kibble, slightly moistened with water. At weeks 6-7, they should be fully able to eat solid food.

Many kittens are fully weaned at around the eighth week, but experts do not recommend separating them from their mother until the 10th-12th week. Throughout this time, during the past twelve weeks, the process of socialization must have been constant and regular. You can progress from short, daily periods of gentle handling to begin with, so that they grow accustomed to your presence. You can assist in weaning them by the 4th week, and should be able to enjoy cuddling and playing with them by the 7th-8th week. If everything has gone well, the kittens should be active, alert, playful, curious, and not timid or shy in your presence. Vaccinations should start at around the 6th-8th week, so the process of socialization should gradually progress as you introduce them to a bigger world and being handled by other people.

Chapter Nine: Showing Your Siberian Cat

The earliest recorded cat show which a Siberian cat was presented was in England in 1871. But it wasn't until 1987 that the first breed standard for the Siberian cat was written and published by the Kotofei Cat Club in St. Petersburg. Since then, the Siberian breed has been accepted and registered by various cat organizations not only in Russia but around the world, and is steadily gaining popularity among pet lovers the world over.

This chapter contains an overview of the breed standards of some of these organizations, including the Cat

Fancier's Association (CFA), Fédération Internationale Féline (FIFe), The International Cat Association (TICA), the Governing Council of Cat Fancy (GCCF), and the American Cat Fancier's Association/Cat Aficionado Association (ACFA/CAA). And finally, we look at some practical tips and guides on how best to prepare yourself and your Siberian for a cat show.

A General Overview of Siberian Cat Breed Standards

It is good to remember that in a cat show, cats do not necessarily compete against each other, and nor is it a competition to see which cat is better than all the rest. Rather, cats are shown to determine how closely they adhere to the show organization's written breed standard. That is why it is always a good idea to be very familiar with the breed standard of the organization whose show you are aiming to join.

Below we have provided you an overview of the breed standards of some of the major cat organizations in the world. You will notice that while there are no great differences when it comes to breed standards, there are some differences, as well as standards that are considered acceptable in some, but not acceptable in others. Most also consider allowances for the breed's slow maturation (taking about five years to mature), and the comparative smaller size of the females compared to the males.

1. Cat Fancier's Association (CFA)Breed Standard for Siberian Cats

General:

Siberians are medium to medium large cat, strong, with a triple coat. Overall appearance is of strength, presence, alertness, and a sweet facial expression. A general impression of roundness and circles.

Head

The head is of a modified wedge with rounded contours, broader at the top of the skull, but narrowing slightly to a full-rounded muzzle. There is a slight doming between the ears and an almost flat area on the forehead. Transition between the side of the head and the muzzle is gentle and inconspicous.

Ears

The ears are medium-large, rounded, wide at the base and tilting slightly forward. The hair is short and thin over the back of the ears, and furnishings are long from the middle of the ear, covering the base of the ear. Ear tipping is allowed.

Eyes

The eyes are medium to large, almost round. They should be open, alert, and expressive. There is no relationship between eye color and coat color/pattern, except for blue eyes for color points.

Neck and Body

The neck is rounded, sturdy, and well-muscled. The body is medium in legnth, well-muscled, with the back slightly arched and higher than the shoulders. The belly is firm and barrel-shaped. Moderate stomach pads or famine pouch on the lower abdomen is acceptable.

Legs, Feet and Tail

The legs are medium in length, with substantial boning, the hind legs slightly longer than the front legs.

The feet are big and rounded, toe tufts are considered desirable.

The tail is medium in length, a bit shorter than the length of the body. It is wide at the base, tapering to a blunt tip, even and thickly furnished.

Coat, Coat Color, and Coat Patterns

The coat is moderately long to long, with a triple coat. The hair on the shoulderblades and lower part of the chest is thick but slightly shorter. There is an abundant fur collar ruff, and the hair on the belly and britches may thicken to curls. Wavy coats are not characteristic. The texture can vary from coarse to soft, depending on the color, and on the season.

All colors, color combinations and patterns are accepted, with or without white. Buttons, spots and lockets are also allowed, though strong and clear patterns are considered desirable.

Temperament

The temperament must be unchallenging.

Penalties and Disqualifications

The following are penalized: straight profile, narrow or fox-like muzzle, long tail, delicate boning, non-muscular, almond-shaped eyes, long or short legs, a long body, and lack of good body weight.

Disqualifications are considered for kinked tails, incorrect number of toes, crossed eyes, and evidence of illness, poor health, and emaciation.

2. Fédération Internationale Féline (or FIFe) Siberian Cat Breed Standard

General

The Siberian is a medium to large cat, with females mostly smaller than males.

Head

The head is a bit longer than it is broad, softly rounded, and massive. The cheekbones are well developed, the nose is medium in length, broad, with a slight indentation but without a stop.

Ears

The ears are medium in size, tilting slightly forward, and with a good width in between. The tips are rounded with well-developed hairs inside, and tufts.

Eyes

The eyes are large, slightly oval in shape, a bit oblique, and set widely apart. Clear eye color is desired. Any color is permitted; there is no relationship between eye color and coat color, except for blue for NEMs, the more intensive, the better.

Legs, Body and Tail

The legs are medium high, strong, and forms a rectangle with the body. The paws are large, round, and well-tufted between the toes.

The body is well boned and well muscled, with a powerful neck broad chest, and in proportion , creating a rectangular appearance.

The tail is medium in length, thick, with a rounded tip. It is covered by dense hair, with no hairs trailing down.

Coat

The coat is semi-long, dense, the undercoat not lying flat, the overcoat water repellent, and slightly hard to the touch.

The summer coat is shorter than the winter coat. The wintercoat has a well-developed shirt front, full frill, and knickerbockers.

All color varieties, including with white, are permitted, except pointed patterns, chocolate and lilac, cinnamon and fawn. Any amount of white is permitted, including white blaze, white locket, white chest, white on the belly, white on the paws, etc.

Allowed color point varieties for NEM are seal, blue, red, cream, seal/blue tortie, smoke, tabby and/or silver golden. These are also allowed with white. Colorpoint varieties not allowed are chocolate, lilac, fawn, and cinnamon.

Faults

The following are considered faults: a body that is too small or too finely built, long and narrow head, too round head, too large or too high set ears, round eyes, too long or too thin legs, too short tail, too fine or silky coat, a coat that lies flat, and a lack of coat (except in the summer).

3. The International Cat Association's (TICA) Siberian Cat Breed Standards

General

The Siberian is a medium-large cat, strong and powerful, with a sweet facial expression. The general impression is of circles and roundness. Allowances are made for slow maturation.

Head and Ears

The head is medium/large in size, of a modified wedge shape, with rounded contours. It is broader at the top of the skull, narrowing slightly to a full-rounded muzzle. The cheekbones are neither high set nor prominent. The chin is well-rounded, not protruding, and is line with the nose. The muzzle is short, full, and rounded. Transition between the side of the head and muzzle is gentle and inconspicuous.

The ears are medium-large, rounded and tilted slightly forward, set at one and one and a half ear's width apart. The hair over the back of the ear is short and thin, and furnishings are long from the middle of the ear, covering the base of the ear. Lynx tipping is allowed.

Neck and Body

The neck is rounded, substantial and well-muscled.

The torso is medium in length, well-muscled, with the back arched slightly higher than the shoulders. The torso is barrel-shaped, and a firm belly gives the sensation of solid weight.

Legs and Feet

The legs are medium in length, with the hind legs slightly longer than the frong, with substantial boning.

The feet are big and rounded. Toe tufts are desirable.

Tail

The tail is medium in length, wide at the base and tapering slightly to a blunt tip. The tail is somewhat shorter than the length of the body.

Boning and Musculature

The boning is substantial. The musculature is also substantial and powerful.

Coat and Coat Colors and Patterns

The coat is moderately long to long, with a triple coat. The hair on the shoulder blades and lower part of the chest is thicker and slightly shorter. An abundant ruff sets off the head. The tight undercoat is thicker in cold weather. The hair on the belly and britches may thicken to curls, but a wavy coat is not characteristic.

The coat texture varies from coarse to soft, according to color. Clear patterns are desirable.

All colors, traditional and pointed, and combinations, are accepted, with or without white, which are allowed on the chin, breast, and the stomach of tabbies. White is allowed in most areas. Strong colors are desirable.

Temperament

Must be unchallenging.

Penalties

The following are penalized: straight profile, narrow muzzle, long tail, delicate boning, non-muscular body, long body, almond-shaped eyes, very long legs.

Disqualifications and awards withheld

Evidence of illness, poor health, emaciation, visible tail fault.

A sign of definite challenge in temperament disqualifies.

3. **The Siberian Cat Club Standard of Point, affiliated with and recognized by the Governing Council of the Cat Fancy (GCCF)**

General

The Siberian cat is a medium to large semi-longhaired cat. The overall impression should be of substance and rounded contours. The Siberian has a very distinctive weatherproof coat, and should reflect their natural heritage as a natural outdoor cat in Russia. The expression must be alert, and the cat in good general condition and well-presented. No points for color are awarded, so there are no penalties for wrongly registered colors.

Head

The head forms a short, broad wedge with rounded contours, and a slightly rounded muzzle and chin. The lower forehead is slightly domed. The nose should be of uniform width, and the whisker pads moderately well developed and form a gentle, rounded line with the chin. The muzzle is broad and rounded.

The cheekbones are low set, very broad and connected by a gentle, rounded line to the whisker pads and chin, producing a desired impression.

Ears and Eyes

The ears are of medium sized, set wide apart at the width of an ear or more between, with rounded tips. The ears should be well-furnished.

The eyes are large, slightly oval shaped, with a rounded lower line. They are set slightly oblique and wide apart. The color should be clear and bright. Any shade is allowed, except that blue and odd-eyes are allowed in white and van-patterned Siberians, and blue for color pointed Siberians.

Body, Legs and Feet

The body is rectangular but not to long, large, well-muscled, heavily built with a broad chest. The neck is short and substantial.

The legs are of medium length with substantial bone structure and strength.

The paws are large, toes carried close, rounded, and with well-developed tufts.

Tail

The tail is broad at the base, proportionate in length, tapering slightly towards the tip, and should reach the shoulder blade. The tail should be well-furnished.

Coat and Coat Colors and Patterns

The coat is medium-length, with a dense undercoat that is soft, fine, and "springy." The topcoat is coarser and more substantial. The fur over the shoulders is shorter, with smoothly flowing guard hairs over the back, flanks, and upper side of the tail. The hair is firm to the touch and waterproof.

The underside of the body and breeches have only an undercoat which is shorter, dense, and plentiful. Long, plentiful ruff is preferred.

A wide variety of colors and patterns are recognized, including color pointed. The following are not accepted, whether or not in any pattern combination: chocolate, cinnamon, caramel, and dilute colors of lilac, fawn, and apricot. Burmese or Tonkinese colors are not accepted. Any amount of white is allowed. Color pointed varieties are also called Neva Masquerade. Allowances are made for belly spots and shading on color points.

Withholding Awards:

Awards withheld for the following, though judge's discretion is allowed with kittens with respect to numbers 4 and 6 below:

1. narrow, high cheekbones
2. slight or delicate build, fine legs, and oval paws
3. straight profile, definite stop or tapering nose
4. long, triangular, narrow, oval head
5. tail not in proportion to the body
6. soft, silky, or Persian type coat
7. protruding, round or small eyes
8. Any defects listed with the SOP booklet

4. American Cat Fancier's Association (ACFA) Siberian Cat Breed Standard

General

Russia's native cat, the Siberian is a medium to medium-large, strong cat. Overall appearance should be of strength and force, with excellent physical condition and alertness, and a sweet facial expression. Allowances made for slow maturation, males being larger than females, and size differences for young juveniles. The general impression is of roundness and circles, rather than rectangles and triangles.

Head

The head is a modified wedge of medium to medium-large, with rounded contours, broader at the skull, narrowing slightly to a slightly rounded short muzzle, with noticeable whisker pads. Cheekbones are neither high set nor prominent, but apparent. Top of the head is flat, the nose has a gentle concave curve, a slight doming between the ears, and an almost flat area on the forehead.

The chin is well rounded, not protruding, and in line with the nose.

Ears and Eyes

The ears are medium, wide at the base, set at a minimum of 1 to 1/2 ear width apart. Tips are rounded and ears are tilted forward. Lynx tipping is preferred. Hair over the back of the ears is short and thin, furnishings are long and covers the base completely. The inner ear has an abundance of ear tufts.

The eyes are moderately large, rounded, and wide set. Acceptable eye colors covers the green, blue-green, gold, hazel, or copper spectrum. Blue or odd-eyed are allowed in white or "-and white" cats. The eyes are blue in color points.

Neck and Body

The neck is medium, rounded, substantial, and well-muscled.

The body is medium in length, well muscled, with the back arched and slightly higher than the shoulders. The body is barrel-shaped, and a firm belly gives the sensation of solid weight.

Legs, Feet and Tail

The legs are thick and dense and medium in length. The feet are big and round. Toe tufts are desirable.

The tail is medium somewhat shorter than the length of the body. It is wide at the base, blunt at the tip, without any thickening or kinks. The tail should be evenly and thickly furnished.

Coat and Coat Colors

The coat is plush, medium length. The hair on the shoulder blades and the lower part of the chest are thick and slightly shorter. There is a ruff setting the head, a tight undercoat which is thicker on cold weather. The hair may thicken to curls (not waves) on the belly and britches. The skin may have a bluish cast. Clear and strong colors and patterns are desirable. Coat texture may vary with color.

Accepted coat colors and patterns are those registered by the ACFA.

For Point patterns, the points of ears, legs, feet, tail, and mask should show the cat's basic color. The body color is lighter than point color, and the chest, bib and chin may be lighter in color. All Pointed cats have blue eye color.

For Pointed & White, the points of ear, mask and tail must be well-defined. The mask is a white inverted "V." The stomach, all four legs, feet, and ruff are white, and the body color is a shade lighter than poitns. May have various white markings and color patches. The nose leather and paw pads are pink.

Penalties and Withholding

The following are penalized: adult cats not having substantial weight, straight profile, narrow or fox-like muzzle, almond-shaped eyes, very long legs, thin legs, and small ears.

Awards withheld in case of the following: white on points, white on ears and tail for Pointed & White, including dark markings on white area of the mask.

Preparing Your Siberian Cat for Show

Joining a cat show and entering your Siberian for show can be both a fun and educational experience. Not only do you learn more about the Siberian breed, but in implementing best practices in nutrition, grooming, diet, and training in preparation for the show, you can strengthen the bond between yourself and your pet in a very big way.

Cat shows are usually divided into four categories: kitten, championship, premiership, and household pets. While the first three only accepts pedigreed cats, the Household Pets (HHP)category also accepts altered and mixed-breed cats of known or unknown heritage. This is a good starting point for novice show cats and their owners as they learn the ropes, as there is also less stress and competition within the HHP category.

Preparation for a cat show can take some time. First of all, it is a good idea to begin attending some of these shows just to see what happens, how it works, and to network with other cat enthusiasts. And don't forget to do your research. You will likely begin by joining the cat show nearest to your area, but remember that most cat organizations adhere to different written breed standards. See if you can obtain a written copy of the organization's Siberian cat breed standard to begin with, as well as a copy of their rules and regulations when it comes to joining a show. Most likely, aside from papers to fill up, there will be fees to pay. And of course, pay particular attention to the standard's rules on categories, disqualifications, or penalties. It has happened that gorgeous cats who join shows don't snag a prize simply because they were registered in the wrong category, or possessed certain traits that were disqualified. For instance, while there are some that allow declawing, others, like the CFA, do not. And certain coat markings or colored are not considered for Siberian breeds. That is why you should go through the breed standard carefully, objectively assessing your cat in light of what the judges will look for, before you even attempt to join a show. As you attend more shows, try to observe which cats the judges pick as winners, and why you think they have decided that these cats represent the best of their breed.

If you decide that your Siberian cat does have the potential to be a true show cat, it is time to prepare in earnest. There is the regular grooming, proper diet and nutrition, medical health checks, and socialization and conditioning to prepare your Siberian for the big day.

Remember that in most shows, demonstrating a challenging temperament can be considered a fault, or in some instances, an outright disqualification. There are many who decide on their cats being show cats early on, from kittenhood, and preparation begins as early as then. After all, proper temperament is something that is acquired after a lifetime of nurturing, love, affection, and enough exposure to strange situations and people.

As you get nearer to the big day, you may want to bring your cat along for some of the other shows you are not joining. This allows you to assess how your Siberian would react in the unique environment of a show hall - with the mixture of different people and different cats all gathered together in one room. If your cat is easily spooked, perhaps he isn't quite ready yet.

It is a good idea to begin preparations in earnest at least three months before the show itself. First of all, see to the paperwork. Most shows require that you fill up paperwork and send it in duly filled. They might also require that your cat be healthy and vaccinated, so secure these documents early on from your veterinarian. Submit all of these well ahead of time so that you have some leeway in case they ask for something else or there are things you have to double-check. And of course, don't forget to pay the fees, and make sure you have a copy of the receipt. Make copies of all these documents for yourself, and put them aside in a secure place.

Groom your Siberian regularly, and make sure he is eating well and is in perfect health and condition. Try to get him used to being handled by strangers at different times. The judges will likely be feeling their bodies, examining their tail, teeth, their undersides, so this is a good way to condition them for the show. Do this in a positive atmosphere and environment, and reward them for behaving properly so that when it is time for the show, it won't be quite so novel for your Siberian cat.

As you approach nearer the date of the show, here is a checklist of a few things you should remember:

- Make sure you have enough money with you. Aside from the costs of entering the show, you are sometimes also given the option of paying extra for cage space, grooming space, and end of row benching. Factor in the costs of transportation, the equipment you will be bringing with you, and the cost of your own needs (such as food, water, and if the show is out of town, lodgings).
- Don't forget to bring your cat's registration papers, confirmation letter, vaccination documents, a copy of the show's rules and regulations, and proof of payments with you.

- Make a checklist of the things you will need to bring with you for the show to make sure you have everything you need. Include grooming supplies, food and water bowls, food and water, medicine should it be needed, a pet bed and carrier, litter and a litter box, garbage bags for your trash, show curtains to line the inside of the cage, and clips to hold the curtains in place, and some of his favorite toys to keep him occupied while waiting.

- You will likely not be allowed to leave the show prior to judging, or at least until the show is finished, so it will be quite a wait for you. Bring along extra clothes, food and water for yourself, and make sure you are wearing comfortable shoes.

If you have prepared well in advance, you should be able to relax the night before the show and during the show itself. Don't forget to have fun, to make new friends, and remember that the event is a celebration of the beauty and uniqueness of each individual cat!

Chapter Ten: Keeping Your Siberian Cat Healthy

Siberian cats are survivors - they evolved naturally in the severe climate of Russia, adapting to survive, and nature itself has weaned out those who were unable to endure the

Russian winter, or were unable to catch prey for food. Human intervention only came in in terms of selective breeding during the late 1980s, but of course by then, they had a pretty good stock to work with. Siberian cats, after all, managed to survive admirably on their own for centuries.

But while Siberians are hardy and generally healthy breed, they do seem prone to one genetic condition: hypertrophic cardiomyopathy. It is always best to get a kitten from a reputable breeder as this reduces the risks of your getting a kitten prone to HCM, but remember there is no 100% health guarantee, even among the most conscientious of Siberian breeders.

Hypertrophic Cardiomyopathy (HCM)

HCM in cats is possibly caused by genetic mutations and predispositions among carriers, but the precise cause is still unknown.

HCM occurs when the left ventricle of the heart, which is responsible for receiving and pumping oxygenated blood into the aortic valve, which blood is then circulated throughout the rest of the body, is compromised. Normally, the left ventricle is already thick due to its work of receiving blood from the lungs before pumping it out again for distribution to the rest of the body. But in HCM, the left ventricle is abnormally enlarged or thickened.

When this happens, the volume of the chamber through which the blood passes is decreased, and this can result in an increased heart rate as a reflex in order to maintain blood pressure and cardiac output. The heart is thus overworked, compromising its overall function. HCM is the most commonly diagnosed cardiac disease in cats, and the most common cause of heart failure.

Some of the signs and symptoms to watch out for include:

- lethargy
- difficulty breathing
- short, rough or snapping sounds during breathing
- abnormal heart sounds (i.e., heart murmur, gallop rhythm, abnormalities in the heart rate, or cardiac dysrrhythmias)
- inability to tolerate exercise
- sudden hind-limb paralysis (this is caused by blood clots that block vessels or thromboembolism, usually in the periprheral circulation such as the hind legs. Pain may also be observed in the hind legs.)
- bluish discoloration of the foot pads and nailbeds caused by insufficient oxygen
- cold extremities such as the ears and the paws, due to poor circulation
- collapse
- sudden heart failure

- loss of appetite
- weak pulse

Detecting the symptoms may not always be easy, especially in cats which are comparatively less active than dogs. And some cats may not show signs of illness, especially during the early stages of the disease. This is why it is important to bring in your cat for a veterinary checkup at least twice a year. During the examination, the more telling symptoms may be revealed, such as a heart murmur or irregular heart rhythm. If HCM is suspected, diagnosis can be confirmed through chest x-rays, an ECG (electrocardiogram), and an echocardiagram (heart ultrasound). The latter, or the echocardiogram, is most useful in a visual examination of the heart for signs of enlargement or thickening of the walls. A defitive diagnosis can be made once other possible causes such as hyptertension and hyperthyroidism are ruled out. It is recommended that ultrasound examinations be repeated every six months to monitor the progress of the disease, and to determine any modifications in treatment.

Treatment of HCM depends on the severity of the disease and its clinical manifestations. Some of the medications that may be prescribed are commonly to help with the following:

- beta-adrenergic blockers to help slow the heart rate

- calcium-channel blockers to lessen the incidence of arrhythmic activity and possible ventricular relaxing effect
- diuretics to control edema and effusions
- anti-coagulants to decrease the chances of blood clot formation

The effect of medication is variable, and it really depends on the severity of the disease and its manifestations. Should HCM be diagnosed early, however, medication may help to slow or delay the progression of this condition.

Should your cat be suffering from congestive heart failure, hospitalizaton and oxygen therapy in case of difficulty breathing is advised, as well as confinement in a warm and quiet environment with minimal stress.

That said, medication should always go hand in hand with some form of therapy to help the cat adjust to the unique needs and requirements of his condition. This would usually include a no-sodium diet and a stress-free environment to minimize excitement and stress on the heart.

HCM usually occurs in cats 5-7 years of age, though it has not been unheard of in kittens as young as 3 months old. Prognosis is also quite variable, as some cats may go for years without showing any clinical signs. It is usually a progressive condition, however. But while it can shorten a cat's lifespan, appropriate therapy and early diagnosis and treatment can allow many cats a longer and improved quality of life.

Preventing Illness with Vaccinations

It is essential to have your kitten vaccinated to enable their immune system to fight against some of the more prevalent and dangerous diseases to which felines are prone to. This is particularly important for kittens, whose immune systems are not yet fully developed. In general, six-week old kittens can begin receiving vaccinations.

As soon as you bring your kitten to the veterinarian for a check-up, ask about the recommended vaccine schedule. Your vet should explain to you that there are two different types of vaccines: core and non-core vaccines. While core vaccinations are essential as they protect against diseases that are common and prevalent among the cat population, there is a certain leeway when it comes to non-core vaccinations. Depending on the risks of infection in terms of geographic location, local environment, or lifestyle, sometimes the vaccination itself may actually pose a higher risk than not being vaccinated at all. Recent debates have made pet owners dubious of the effectivity of non-core vaccinations because too much vaccination may actually cause unintended side-effects or adverse reactions. Of course, should certain diseases be prevalent in a certain geographic area, non-core vaccinations may be strongly recommended by your vet.

Core vaccinations are recommended for Rabies, Feline Viral Rhinotracheitis (FVR), Feline Calicivirus (FCV), and Feline Panleukopenia (FPV). These last three are usually offered in a combination vaccine that is administered as early as six weeks, and repeated every 3-4 weeks until the kitten reaches 16 weeks or older. Rabies vaccine is usually administered at 8-12 weeks, depending on the vaccine.

Non-core vaccinations include: [Rabies (in certain areas)], Chlamydohila felis, Feline Leukemia virus (FeLV), Feline immunodeficiency virus (FIV), and Bordetella.

The following vaccines are *not* recommended for safety issues and questionable effectiveness: Feline Infectious Peritonitis (FIP), and Giardia Lamblia.

The following table shows a general core vaccination schedule for kittens starting at 6-8 weeks of age. Please remember that this is only a general guideline for a vaccination schedule. Non-core vaccines may also be recommended by your veterinarian depending on the region where you live.

Core vaccinations will also need to be boostered after one year, and then depending on the vaccine used, every one to three years afterwards.

Age	Core Vaccines
6-8 weeks	FVRCP Vaccine (Feline Viral Rhinotracheitis Calicivirus and Panleukopenia) Also recommended to start Heartworm Prevention
9-12 weeks	FVRCP Booster FELV Vaccine (Feline Leukemia Virus)
16 weeks	FVRCP Booster FELV Booster Rabies Vaccine

** Keep in mind that vaccine requirements may vary from one region to another. Only your vet will be able to tell you which vaccines are most important for the region where you live.

Siberian Cat Care Sheet

This section bring together some of the pertinent information presented throughout this book, giving you a comprehensive overview and summary of some of the finer points about Siberian Cats. You can read this section first as a starting point before going through the rest of this book, or you can simply refer to the information below from time to time, or as needed. Some of the information presented below include basic information about Siberian cats, their nutritional and health needs, and breeding information.

1.) Basic Siberian Cat Information

Pedigree: the result of careful breeding and development of the erstwhile natural "Siberian" cats that were well-known for years in Russia

Breed Size: medium to large size

Weight: 4-10 kg. (8.8-22 lbs.)

Body Type: hefty; solid and muscular

Coat Length: moderate to long, heavy triple coat

Coat Texture: can be soft or very coarse; longer and thicker fur on the shoulders and chest, curly but not wavy coat on the legs and belly, and a full mane on the chest

Color: wide variety of colors and patterns

Eyes: large, slightly oval in shape, but with a rounded lower line, set wide apart and are slightly oblique; colors can range from coppers to greens, and blue in Neva Masquerade varieties

Ears: medium to large, wide-set, rounded tips with a forward tilt; tufts of fur from the inside of the ears and on the tips, giving them "lynx tips"

Tail: medium length, wide at the base and with a blunt tip; thickly covered with fur from the base to the tip

Temperament: loyal, affectionate, friendly and playful, often being described as having a "dog-like temperament

Strangers: friendly with strangers

Children: very good with children

Other Pets: gets along with dogs and most other pets

Exercise Needs: needs some daily exercise, either playing or walking

Health Conditions: generally healthy but prone to Hypertrophic cardiomyopathy (HCM), Polycystic Kidney Disease (PKD)

Lifespan: wide range, average 11 to 15 years

2.) Nutritional Needs

Nutritional Needs: water, protein, carbohydrate, fats, vitamins, minerals

Calorie Needs: varies by age, weight, and activity level

Amount to Feed (kitten): feed freely but consult recommendations on the package

Amount to Feed (adult): consult recommendations on the package; calculated by weight

Feeding Frequency: four to five small meals daily

Important Ingredients: fresh animal protein (chicken, beef, lamb, turkey, eggs), animal fats, digestible carbohydrates (rice, oats, sweet potato)

Important Minerals: calcium, copper, iodine, manganese, magnesium, potassium, selenium, zinc, and phosphorus

Important Vitamins: Vitamin A, Vitamin C, Vitamin B, Vitamin D, Vitamin E, Vitamin K

Look For: AAFCO statement of nutritional adequacy; protein at top of ingredients list; no artificial flavors, dyes, preservatives

3.) Breeding Information

Sexual Maturity (female): average 5 to 6 months

Sexual Maturity (male): 8 to 9 months

Breeding Age (female): 12 months, ideally 18 to 24 months

Breeding Age (male): at least 18 months

Breeding Type: seasonally polyestrous, multiple cycles per year

Ovulation: induced ovulation, stimulated by breeding

Litter Size: 5-6 kittens

Pregnancy: average 63 days

Kitten Birth Weight: 80 to 100 grams (0.2 to 0.22 lbs.)

Characteristics at Birth: eyes and ears closed, little to no fur, completely dependent on mother

Eyes/Ears Open: 8 to 12 days

Teeth Grow In: around 3 to 4 weeks

Begin Weaning: around 4 to 6 weeks, kittens are fully weaned by 8 weeks

Socialization: between 8 and 13 weeks, ready to be separated by 14 weeks

Index

A

B

C

X

Y

Photo References

Page 1 Photo by Romi via Pixabay.
<https://pixabay.com/en/cat-siberian-forest-cat-forest-cat-1390694/>

Page 9 Photo by skeeze via Pixabay.
<https://pixabay.com/en/cat-portrait-domestic-cute-pet-1107338/>

Page 19 Photo by Couleur via Pixabay.
<https://pixabay.com/en/cat-red-tomcat-mieze-lying-meadow-1319044/>

Page 29 Photo by Jonathane via Wikimedia Commons.
<https://commons.wikimedia.org/wiki/File:Siberian_cat.JPG>

Page 41 Photo by Gatto Siberiano Murmur's via Wikimedia Commons.
<https://commons.wikimedia.org/wiki/File:Murmur%27s_Siberian_Cat_siberiano_golden.JPG>

Page 45 Photo by DorotaGieranczyk via Wikimedia Commons.
<https://commons.wikimedia.org/wiki/File:My_cute_siberian_cat,_Yoggi.jpg>

Page 55 Photo by Roswitha BuddeCattery vom Hohen Timp via Wikimedia Commons. <https://commons.wikimedia.org/wiki/File:Siberian_cat_in _summercoat.JPG>

Page 61 Photo by Joesadlon via Wikimedia Commons. <https://commons.wikimedia.org/wiki/File:KIKI_Neva_Ma squerade.jpg>

Page 69 Photo by Southernseas via Wikimedia Commons. <https://commons.wikimedia.org/wiki/File:Colorpoint_Sib erian_Kittens_at_13_Weeks.JPG>

Page 83 Photo by Руслан Степаненко via Wikimedia Commons. <https://commons.wikimedia.org/wiki/File:%D0%92%D0%B 5%D1%82%D0%B5%D1%80%D0%BE%D0%BA_%D0%A1% D0%B8%D0%B1%D0%B5%D1%80%D0%B8%D1%8F.jpg>

Page 105 Photo by Avelesik via Wikimedia Commons. <https://commons.wikimedia.org/wiki/File:Murka.jpg>

Page 113 Photo by Mstachul via Wikimedia Commons. <https://commons.wikimedia.org/wiki/File:Siberian_cat_- _Tofik.jpg#>

References

"About the Siberian." CFA.
<http://cfa.org/breeds/breedssthrut/siberian.aspx>

"About the Siberian Cat Breed." About Cat Breeds.
<http://www.aboutcatbreeds.com/about-siberian-cat-breed>

"All About Cat Shows." Jane McGrath.
<http://animals.howstuffworks.com/pets/cat-show4.htm>

"Breed Profile: Getting to Know the Siberian." Cats Center Stage.
<http://www.catscenterstage.com/breeds/siberian2.shtml>

"Breeding and Caring For Your Pregnant Cat." Ron Hines DVM PhD.
<http://www.2ndchance.info/pregnantcatcare.htm>

"Buying a Cat Cost." cost helper pets & pet care.
<http://pets.costhelper.com/buy-cat.html>

"Buying a Siberian Cat: Is it Worth It?" Kim Harris.
<http://www.mnn.com/family/pets/blogs/buying-a-siberian-cat-is-it-worth-it>

"Cardiomyopathy (Heart Disease) in Cats. International Cat Care. <http://icatcare.org/advice/cat-health/cardiomyopathy-heart-disease-cats>

"Caring for Kittens Until they are Weaned." PetWave. <http://www.petwave.com/Cats/Basics/Breeding/Weaning.aspx>

"Caring for Your Cat's Ears." cattime.com. <http://cattime.com/cat-facts/lifestyle/499-caring-for-your-cats-ears>

"Cat Breeding - Is It For You?" Pets4Homes. <http://www.pets4homes.co.uk/pet-advice/cat-breeding-is-it-for-you.html>

"Cat-Proof Your Home in 12 Easy Steps." The Humane Society of the United States. <http://www.humanesociety.org/animals/cats/tips/cat_proofing_your_house.html>

"Cat Showing FAQ Part I: Deciding to Show." Barbara French, Tarantara Cattery. <http://www.fanciers.com/other-faqs/show-faq-pt1.html>

"Characteristics of a Siberian Cat." Maura Wolf, Demand Media. <http://pets.thenest.com/characteristics-siberian-cat-4605.html>

"Ear Care and Ear Problems in Cats." WebMD.
    <http://pets.webmd.com/cats/guide/cat-ear-care-
    problems>

"Feeding Your Siberian." Glorious Siberians.
    <http://glorioussiberians.com/feeding-siberian/>

"Feline Estrous Cycle." BreedingCats.com.
    <http://www.breeding-cats.com/estrous-cycle.html>

"Feline Heat Cycle." Revival Animal Health.
    <http://www.revivalanimal.com/articles/Feline-Heat-
    Cycles.html>

"Feline Pregnancy." BreedingCats.com.
    <http://www.breeding-cats.com/felinepregnancy.html>

"Feline Vaccination." Wikipedia.
    <https://en.wikipedia.org/wiki/Feline_vaccination>

"Food." Mystic Melody.
    <http://www.siberiancat.com/food.html>

"Grooming." Mystic Melody.
    <http://www.siberiancat.com/grooming.html>

"Grooming." Pedigree Siberian Cat Association.
    <http://www.pedigreesiberiancatassociation.com/groomi
    ng>

"Grooming." Rare Siberian Cats.
    <http://www.raresiberiancats.com/grooming.html>

"Guidelines for simple commands and tricks." Petzine.org. <http://www.petzine.org/cats/training-behaviour-cats/guidelines-for-simple-commands-and-trick>

"Heart Disease (Hypertrophic Cardiomyopathy) in Cats. PetMD. <http://www.petmd.com/cat/conditions/cardiovascular/c_ct_cardiomyopathy_hypertrophic#>

"History of Siberian Cats." Sibirskiy Cattery. <http://sibirskiy.com/siberian_history>

"History of the Siberian Cat." Mystic Melody Siberians. <http://www.siberiancat.com/about-the-siberian-cat.html>

"How Long are Cats in Heat For?" Janet Tobiassen Crosby, DVM. <http://vetmedicine.about.com/od/pregnancybirthincats/f/Cat_estrus.htm>

"How long is a cat in heat?" Animal Planet. <http://www.animalplanet.com/pets/how-long-is-a-cat-in-heat/>

"How to choose a breeder." Siberian Cats Bolshoydom. <http://www.siberiancats-canada.com/how-to-select-a-breeder.html>

"How to Groom a Siberian Cat." The Nest. <http://pets.thenest.com/groom-siberian-cat-7166.html>

"How to socialize a Hypoallergenic Siberian Cat?" Forest Dreams Cattery. <http://www.hypoallergeniccats.co.uk/#!How-to-socialize-a-Hypoallergenic-Siberian-Cat/c1fou/55755ab30cf2df2eae3a71ea>

"How to tell if a cat is pregnant." Purina. <https://www.purina.co.uk/cats/key-life-stages/pregnancy/spotting-the-signs-of-cat-pregnancy>

"How to Train a Cat: Tips and Tricks." Dr. Joanne Righetti. <http://www.purina.com.au/cats/training/train>

"Human Foods that are poisonous to cats." Vetsnow. <https://www.vets-now.com/pet-owners/cat-care-advice/human-foods-poisonous-cats/>

"Hypertrophic Cardiomyopathy (HCM). Cornell University College of Veterinary Mecidine. <http://vet.cornell.edu/hospital/Services/Companion/Cardiology/conditions/HCM.cfm>

"Hypertrophic Cardiomyopathy (HCM). O.L. Nelson, DVM, Diplomate ACVIM. <https://www.vetmed.wsu.edu/outreach/Pet-Health-Topics/categories/diseases/hypertrophic-cardiomyopathy-in-cats>

"Kitten Development from Birth to Eight Weeks." BreedingCats.com. <http://www.breeding-cats.com/kitten-development.html>

"Kitten Proof Your Home." Purina. <http://www.purina.com.au/kittens/new-kitten/proof-your-home>

"Kitten Vaccinations." BreedingCats.com. <http://www.breeding-cats.com/kitten-vaccinations.html>

"Labour and giving birth." Purina. <https://www.purina.co.uk/cats/key-life-stages/pregnancy/cat-labour-and-giving-birth>

"Managing Fertility of Your Queen." BreedingCats.com. <http://www.breeding-cats.com/managing-fertility.html>

"Mistakes People Make Feeding Cats." WebMD. <http://pets.webmd.com/cats/guide/mistakes-people-make-feeding-cats>

"Should I brush my cat's teeth?" Forest Wind Siberian Cats. <http://www.forestwind-siberian-cats.com/apps/blog/show/26260537-should-i-brush-my-cat-s-teeth->

"Should I Get a Cat? Weighing the Pros Cons and Costs of Getting a Cat." Sydney.

<http://untemplater.com/untemplate/should-i-get-a-cat-weighing-the-pros-cons-and-costs-of-getting-a-cat/>

"Siberian." ACFA. <http://www.acfacat.com/Breed%20Standards/SIBERIAN.pdf>

"Siberian." cattime. <http://cattime.com/cat-breeds/siberian-cats>

"Siberian." CFA. <http://cfa.org/Portals/0/documents/breeds/standards/siberian.pdf>

"Siberian." Embrace Pet Insurance. <http://www.embracepetinsurance.com/cat-breeds/siberian>

"Siberian." FIFe. <http://www1.fifeweb.org/dnld/std/SIB-NEM.pdf>

"Siberian." TICA. <http://www.tica.org/cat-breeds/item/269-siberian-introduction>

"Siberian." Vetstreet. <http://www.vetstreet.com/cats/siberian#history>

"Siberian (SB)." TICA. <http://tica.org/pdf/publications/standards/sb.pdf>

"Siberian Cat." Wikipedia. <https://en.wikipedia.org/wiki/Siberian_cat>

"Siberian Cats." Veterinary Pet Insurance.
<http://www.petinsurance.com/healthzone/pet-articles/pet-breeds/Siberian-Cats.aspx>

"Siberian Cat Breed Profile." Your Cat.
<http://www.yourcat.co.uk/Cat-Breed-Profiles/siberian-cat-breed-profile.html>

"Siberian cat breeders, how to know if you have found a good one." Druzhina Siberians.
<http://wwwdruzhinasiberians.blogspot.com/2014/07/siberian-cat-breeders-how-to-know-if.html>

"Siberian Forest Cat History." Diana Fineran & Marion Susan Majdiak.
<http://www.breeds.traditionalcats.com/breedinfo/faqtsiberianfcat/faqtsiberianforestcat.htm>

"Slideshow: Foods Your Cat Should Never Eat." WebMD.
<http://pets.webmd.com/cats/ss/slideshow-foods-your-cat-should-never-eat>

"Socializing your Kitten." Cattime.com.
<http://cattime.com/cat-facts/kittens/82-kitten-socialization>

"Standard of Point." The Siberian Cat Club.
<http://www.siberian-cat-club.co.uk/file/192>

"The Feline Heat Cycle." Drs. Foster & Smith Educational Staff. <http://www.drsfostersmith.com/pic/article.cfm?aid=2904>

"The Healthiest Diet For Your Cat." Dr. Karen Becker. <http://www.huffingtonpost.com/dr-karen-becker/healtthy-cat-diet_b_865604.html>

"The Siberian." Pet Health Network. <http://www.pethealthnetwork.com/cat-health/cat-breeds/siberian>

"The Siberian Cat." Siberian Cat Club. <http://www.siberian-cat-club.co.uk/view/2>

"The Siberian Cat Breed." Snowgum Siberians. <http://www.siberiankittens.com.au/SiberianCats.html>

"The Siberian Cat - The History of Love and Public Recognition." Dr. Irina Sadovnikova, WCF. <https://pawpeds.com/pawacademy/general/siberiancat/>

"Vaccinating Your Kitten." PetMD. <http://www.petmd.com/cat/centers/kitten/health/evr_ct_kitten_vaccination_schedule>

"Weaning Kittens: How and When." PetMD. <http://www.petmd.com/cat/centers/kitten/nutrition/evr_ct_weaning_kittens_what_to_feed_a_kitten>

"What to Expect When Your Cat is Pregnant." WebMD.
    <http://pets.webmd.com/cats/cat-pregnancy-gestation>

Feeding Baby
Cynthia Cherry
978-1941070000

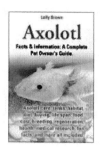

Axolotl
Lolly Brown
978-0989658430

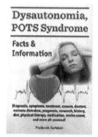

Dysautonomia, POTS
Syndrome
Frederick Earlstein
978-0989658485

Degenerative Disc
Disease Explained
Frederick Earlstein
978-0989658485

Sinusitis, Hay Fever,
Allergic Rhinitis Explained
Frederick Earlstein
978-1941070024

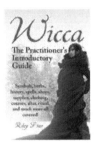

Wicca
Riley Star
978-1941070130

Zombie Apocalypse
Rex Cutty
978-1941070154

Capybara
Lolly Brown
978-1941070062

Eels As Pets
Lolly Brown
978-1941070167

Scabies and Lice Explained
Frederick Earlstein
978-1941070017

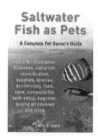

Saltwater Fish As Pets
Lolly Brown
978-0989658461

Torticollis Explained
Frederick Earlstein
978-1941070055

Kennel Cough
Lolly Brown
978-0989658409

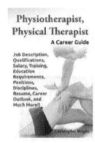

Physiotherapist, Physical
Therapist
Christopher Wright
978-0989658492

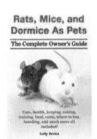

Rats, Mice, and Dormice
As Pets
Lolly Brown
978-1941070079

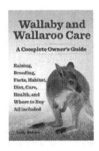

Wallaby and Wallaroo Care
Lolly Brown
978-1941070031

Bodybuilding Supplements
Explained
Jon Shelton
978-1941070239

Demonology
Riley Star
978-19401070314

Pigeon Racing
Lolly Brown
978-1941070307

Dwarf Hamster
Lolly Brown
978-1941070390

Cryptozoology
Rex Cutty
978-1941070406

Eye Strain
Frederick Earlstein
978-1941070369

Inez The Miniature Elephant
Asher Ray
978-1941070353

Vampire Apocalypse
Rex Cutty
978-1941070321

Made in the USA
Lexington, KY
25 September 2018